ACKNOWLEDGMENTS

As you'd expect, a Bible study of this scope could not have happened without the backing of an awesome team. Thank you to the many people who helped bring this project to fruition. They include Mary Huebner, for lending her middle school know-how, and Sean Michael Murphy, for letting us borrow his "talk" expertise. The Youth Specialties/Zondervan team: Heather Campbell, whose tireless efforts and attention to detail made this a better Bible study; Roni Meek, for graciously keeping the team on track; and Jay Howver, for taking seriously the need and desire for depth in youth ministry.

Thank you to my wife, Dana, and the first group of students we ever led through James, a group of college age students ("Zelos") who walked with us through this great book of the Bible and held me accountable in moving from knowing the Word to doing the Word.

Barry Shafer

TABLE OF CONTENTS

Session 5: Faith You Can See (James 2:14-26)

Session 6: Faith You Can Say (James 3:1-12)

Session 7: Wisdom 101 (James 3:13-18)

Session 8: Sanctuary (James 4:1-12)

Session 9: The Time of Your Life (James 4:13-17)

INTRODUCTION

The Bible can be very clear—and very obscure. All of God's Word is valuable. But not all of it is crystal clear in its meaning.

Here's a chance to glean wisdom from one of the most up-front, down-to-earth, meat-and-potatoes books in the Bible—James. It doesn't get any clearer than this New Testament letter.

> So you say you have faith? Let's see it.
>
> Want wisdom? Ask God.
>
> Love money? Prepare for disappointment.
>
> Want results? Pray.

The question can surface as early as middle school and keep surfacing well past the college-age years: *What's God's will for my life?* It's a good question, but it's about three words too long. The real question is: *What's God's will?* As we discover his will, we will know what we're to do with our lives.

And we can start with James.

No book of the Bible comes with more instructions per verse than James. As we invest our lives in this practical to-do list, we'll find ourselves doing God's will.

Through this study students will—

- look under the hood of the trials we suffer and catch a glimpse of why we face these things and how we can overcome them.
- take a good, long look at specific instructions straight from God and set a plan in motion to follow these instructions.
- clear out any elements of favoritism in their lives by searching through some unlikely places where it can hide.
- measure the vital signs of their faith using the gauge supplied by James.
- be challenged to train their tongues to build up rather than tear down.
- take steps toward a power-packed prayer life.

Digging Deeper Series

Today's postmodern students are seeking depth. They are probing Christianity and other faiths, checking to see which faith demands and delivers spiritual depth. The deepest often wins. The Digging Deeper series, a result of collaborative efforts between Youth Specialties and InWord Resources, will give adult leaders everything they need to satisfy their students' craving for depth, while leaving them wanting more of God's Word in their lives. Deeper Bible study has never been more accessible. Or more rewarding.

Every session contains a personal study (Prep It) to guide you, the leader, through the Scripture in a way that still leaves plenty of room for self-discovery. You then choose one of six different session guides (Teach It) from the accompanying CD-ROM. Each guide is targeted for a different age and setting. Leading middle school? Got it! High schoolers at Starbucks? Covered. College age? Got that, too. Need a talk? Here you go. The Teach It guide serves as your cue sheet for navigating the group session.

The Prep It feature helps leaders, whether nervous rookies or seasoned vets, gain competence and confidence in taking on what can appear to be a daunting task: leading students in deeper Bible study. The multiple session options ensure an approach designed specifically for your students.

But there's more. Each study in the Digging Deeper series comes with its own Web support, where you'll find even *more* session options, large-group ideas, user ideas, and constantly updated tie-ins with today's issues and events. You'll also find updated media suggestions (music, video clips) along with specific application and long-term follow-up ideas. You can find this at www.inword. org. Look for the Digging Deeper series icon. We've noted password info for *Hear and Do* in these instructions and throughout the Prep It study guides in this book.

It's a challenge for students to find quality personal time with God in their busy weeks, no matter how much you encourage that activity. The group sessions in the Digging Deeper series come with built-in solitude to help your students explore the great depths of Scripture. This guarantees that for at least a few minutes in their weeks, students are giving God a chance to speak into their lives. With your students fresh off personal discovery, group interaction promises to be invigorating as your students apply in community what they explored in solitude.

You'll soon find that this series offers more than an energizing hour of depth and discussion to help students through their weeks. As students experience God's Word and subtly learn time-tested Bible study tools, they'll lay a solid foundation for confident Bible study and accurate application of Scripture. In short, they'll discover how to listen and respond to God for the rest of their lives.

The intensity of the postmodern student's search for spiritual depth achieves the level of diligent seeking God promises to reward. Built on an inductive Bible study approach, the Digging Deeper series melds that search with God's promise.

INSTRUCTIONS

What You Have Here

Each session contains a guided personal study for the group leader (Prep It) and six different types of session guides (Teach It) for you to choose from, based on the age, and/or setting of your Bible study (middle school, younger high school, older high school, college age, coffeehouse, or a talk). Once you've completed the Prep It, use the session outlines included in this book to choose the appropriate Teach It guide. We've noted descriptions of the guides below. The full Teach It guide for each session, with reproducible student journal pages and Scripture sheets, is on the accompanying CD-ROM.

Prep It

This is a guided personal study for the group leader. Because the most powerful teaching of God's Word flows out of the leader's personal experience in Scripture, this personal prep helps you *own* the Scripture before meeting with your group. The Prep It for each session is included in this book; you'll find plenty of space to write your thoughts and discoveries. Allow about an hour for personal study sometime before the session with your students.

Teach It

Found on the accompanying CD-ROM, the Teach It guide is the leader's cue sheet for leading the session. Teach It includes prompts and notes for moving the group through the exercises, as well as guidance for leading the group discussion. And you have options! Each session has six different Teach It guides from which the leader can choose based on students' ages and the setting of your group time. You'll find the student pages for each session with their respective Teach It guides.

The following design elements will help you navigate through Teach It:

> Some text is in normal type such as you're reading now. This font style indicates instructions and cues to help you move from one exercise to the next during the session.
>
> **Type like this indicates questions, stories, prompts, or points of discussion to raise with your group. You may read these questions word-for-word, or you may**

be more comfortable reframing the questions and points in your own words so you can be more responsive to answers and other comments your students make.

Type like this indicates suggested or sample responses, as well as possible observations from Scripture. In essence, this is the answer font.

This icon found on the student journal pages indicates exercises for students to do in solitude. The Teach It guide contains instructions for the leader to convey to the students before they begin their time alone. The instructions on the students' journal pages will then lead them in a guided personal retreat.

Teach It Descriptions

These descriptions will help you know which Teach It guide is best suited for your group.

- **Middle School:** This session is intended for grades six through eight and is appropriate for a small-group setting or Sunday school.

- **High School 1:** Of the two high school guides, High School 1 is more casual in its approach and is appropriate for high school Sunday school or students who aren't sure how committed they want to be to Bible study and discipleship. It's intended for grades nine through 12, but with a nod toward nine and 10. This guide is also appropriate for the larger teaching settings.

  LARGE-GROUP OPTION:
  In the High School 1 Teach It guides, look for sidebars with the label **Large-Group Option** for ideas on how to lead the session in a large group.

- **High School 2:** This session is intended for the high school student who is looking for depth and has perhaps "signed up" for a deeper experience. It's intended for grades nine through 12, but with a nod toward 11 and 12.

- **College Age:** This session is geared for young adults, whether in college or working a job. The content does assume some spiritual initiative or curiosity on the part of the students.

- **Coffeehouse:** Just what it says—a lighter approach for the coffeehouse or café setting, high school or college age. A couple of suggestions: napkins can make great journal pages, and your servers will appreciate a good tip.

- **Talk:** That's right, a talk guide! And it's just that: a guide. It's not intended to be a manuscript to read aloud. It's here to give you ideas, structure, and stories to blend with your personal study (Prep It) as you prepare a talk. The content complements the other Teach It guides, allowing you to give a talk on the same topic students are studying in other settings (such as small groups). For help with these talks, we brought in an expert, Young Life leader and former area director Sean Michael Murphy. Sean's personal stories are intended to spark your thinking for personal stories of your own. But if nothing "sparks," feel free to simply use one of Sean's stories and intro it by saying, "I read about someone who..."

How This Works

After you've completed the Prep It and chosen the appropriate Teach It guide, print the Teach It guide from the CD-ROM for use in the session. Also print or photocopy enough student pages for your group. Be sure to read through the Teach It guide so you're familiar with the flow of the session and confident with the exercises. This will also help you plan for any exercises that ask for advance preparation.

The Session

An integral part of this study is hands-on interaction with the text by marking key words, promises, instructions, and other phrases—which helps students observe important details they might not uncover with a casual reading. Having bigger text and more space on the included Scripture sheets facilitates this process.

Your students will be using colored pencils to mark the text, so have a good supply available. Most sessions suggest having a couple of colors for each student. While not mandatory, students may find it helpful to use the same color or symbol (or both) from one session to the next when marking the same word or concept.

For example, a student may want to mark all references to God with a blue cloud. Another student may pick a different color but use the same symbol. In most cases we've suggested symbols, but you may want to ask your students for their ideas.

What You'll Need

For every session, you'll need the same basic materials: Bibles, pens, colored pencils, a whiteboard and markers, and copies of Scripture sheets and journal pages. It would be helpful to provide your students with three-ring notebooks for their Scripture sheets and journal pages. Naturally this will add a step to your prep—three-hole punching your student pages for the notebooks. For the coffeehouse setting and the talks, the materials needed will be a bit different.

Some sessions have options that require a few other supplies. It's a good idea to keep a data projector or computer screen handy, since at times you may need to project info or have Web access for video clips.[1] While you can download and play some video clips with a media viewer on your computer (such as Windows Media Player), you'll need to stream other clips from video-sharing Web sites such as YouTube. You'll see suggestions for video clips in the Teach It guides. (Given the temporary nature of Web links, we sometimes list specific links to videos, but also offer useful keywords for Web searches.)

Although we suggest using a whiteboard throughout the book, you can substitute a flip chart, butcher paper taped to the wall, or whatever works conveniently for you.

Web Support

If multiple session guides for you to choose from isn't enough, there's more. You can find additional resources and tie-ins for each session at www.inword.org. Here you'll find up-to-date media suggestions, additional study background, and more session ideas to help you customize the Bible study experience for your students. At www.inword.org look for the Digging Deeper icon and enter the following access information for *Hear and Do* when prompted:

> **username:** Hear
> **password:** Jimmy

Prayer Effort

The purpose of this study isn't to simply fill up the next few Wednesday nights in your student-ministry schedule. It's an opportunity for God to speak to your students through his Word. Therefore, the most important component of your preparation is prayer. We suggest that you organize a group of prayer partners—adults in your student ministry or church—who will pray specifically for your group's experience in this study.

Give these prayer partners the names of your group members, the time frame of the study, and any information that will help them pray specifically for you and your students. In fact, take five minutes now to gather the names and phone numbers of people who have an active prayer life and a heart for the students in your ministry. Then take another 10 minutes to call them, asking them to pray. Commit to staying in touch with your prayer partners, keeping them apprised of your study content and your students' needs. This will also help you stay purposeful in personally praying for your students.

The impact of your Bible study is directly related to the prayer surrounding the study time with your students. We encourage you to make prayer a key part of your personal preparation and your student sessions. God's Spirit is what keeps God's Word from simply being dry words on a page. Open each session asking God's Spirit to soften your students' hearts. Close each session with a commitment to respond to what God has put on each student's heart.

---

1 Before you show video clips to your students, it might be a good idea to check out the Church Video License Web site www.cvli.com/about/index.cfm and Christian Copyright Licensing International www.ccli.com/usa/default.aspx to make sure you are complying with copyright laws.

SESSION 1

Setting the Heart

You're about to spend time doing one of the most important things you can today: preparing to lead teens in a study of God's Word. For the next hour (the estimated amount of preparation time), everything else can wait.

There's a strong possibility—actually, a promise—that the Lord wants to say something to you and your students through the book of James. God promises a reward beyond anything we can imagine when we spend time with him. But don't take my word for it—take his. Before you dive into James, take a moment to soften your heart and clear your mind to hear God's voice. As you read Proverbs 2:1-11 below, note the intense action—the kind of time God asks for when it comes to his Word. Then find the payoff that's promised as a result.

> My son, if you accept my words and store up my commands within you, turning your ear to wisdom and applying your heart to understanding, and if you call out for insight and cry aloud for understanding, and if you look for it as for silver and search for it as for hidden treasure, then you will understand the fear of the LORD and find the knowledge of God. For the LORD gives wisdom, and from his mouth come knowledge and understanding. He holds victory in store for the upright, he is a shield to those whose walk is blameless, for he guards the course of the just and protects the way of his faithful ones. Then you will understand what is right and just and fair—every good path. For wisdom will enter your heart, and knowledge will be pleasant to your soul. Discretion will protect you, and understanding will guard you. (Proverbs 2:1-11)

What an incredible payoff! And aren't the promises in this passage—finding the knowledge of God, understanding every good path, being protected by discretion—benefits you want in your life and the lives of your students? Yet how consistently do we actually *do* what God asks for in these verses? Let this study in James be a step toward storing up, crying out for, looking for, and applying the Word of God. As you study James, not only will you be impacted by its message, but you'll also enjoy the rewards God promises for taking his Word seriously.

Digging In

Will the Real James Please Stand Up?

There's a reasonable chance you know a few things about the book of James. Perhaps that's why you chose this study. But let's start from scratch, assuming we know nothing about who wrote the book and why. Even if you already know this info, your students probably don't. You could simply tell them what you know, but they'd miss the reward of discovering it for themselves. Your group will benefit from digging for the info on their own—and by the way, you will, too.

The New Testament mentions several men named James. Read the following passages, and record the identity or description of each James in the Identity/Description column of the chart.

Matthew 4:21 (James A)
Matthew 10:2-4 (James A and B)
Matthew 13:54-58 (James C)
James 1:1 (James, the author)

Person	Identity/Description	New Info
James A		
James B		
James C		
James, the author		

Is this enough info to conclude who wrote the book of James? Probably not. Here's where a few other Scripture passages can help us out. As the church matured in the years following Jesus' resurrection, several people emerged as leaders. You probably know of Peter, Paul, and John, but a key leader who didn't get as much press was James.

As you read the following passages, write down the new information you learn (or can reasonably infer) about any person named James. If you're able to determine which James the verse refers to, write the facts in the New Info column next to the appropriate name. If you can't relate the info to a specific person, write it in the space provided beneath the corresponding passage.

Acts 1:12-14
This took place just after Jesus left the earth to be with the Father.

Acts 12:1-2

Acts 15:12-23
This was the world's first church board meeting. The apostles, elders, and church leaders met in Jerusalem to decide whether Gentiles should become Jews (and be circumcised) before they became Christians.

Acts 21:17-19
This scene describes Paul's arrival in Jerusalem after his three missionary journeys.

1 Corinthians 15:1-8

Galatians 1:13-19; 2:7-10

Insight

You Say Disciple; I Say Apostle

It may help you to know that people other than Jesus' twelve original disciples are referred to in Scripture as apostles. Barnabas and Paul are both called apostles (Acts 14:14); Paul also writes in 1 Corinthians 15 that Jesus was seen by *the Twelve* and then by all *the apostles*. Based on these apostle sightings in Scripture, when the Bible refers to James as an apostle, it doesn't necessarily refer to one of Jesus' original twelve disciples.

Taking It Inward

Cast Your Vote

Do you see a particular James emerging as a strong candidate as author of the book of James? Here are some key points you may have gathered so far:

- James, the brother of John, is an unlikely candidate since he was killed before the book of James could have been written (Acts 12).
- One James definitely emerged as a pillar (elder and apostle) of the first-century church. This James was a minister to the Jews (Acts 15; Acts 21; 1 Corinthians 15; Galatians 2). James 1:1 indicates the author was addressing a Jewish audience.
- Jesus' half brother James emerged as a pillar (elder and apostle) of the first-century church (Acts 1; Galatians 1).

Who do you think authored the book of James?

☐ James, brother of John, son of Zebedee

☐ James, son of Alphaeus

☐ James, half brother of Jesus

If you checked "James, half brother of Jesus," you agree with the most widely held conclusion regarding the authorship of the New Testament book of James.

Cross-Checking

Now That's a Conversion!

Read John 7:1-5 for another piece of info to throw into the mix. What do you learn about Jesus' brothers?

If Jesus' half brother James was included in this scene (and we have no reason to think he wasn't), he made a big leap from nonbeliever to author of a New Testament letter! But isn't that just like God? Just a little something to keep in mind as you explore his letter.

Digging Deeper

Being a Christian Wasn't Easy Then, Either

Now that we have a feel for who wrote the book of James, we can better understand why he wrote it—and the better we understand the context of a book, the more accurately and powerfully we can apply God's message.

Using your Scripture sheets, read the first chapter of James. As you read, underline any clues about James' audience and what they were facing. It may help you to know that James often introduced a new subject with the phrase *my brothers*.

By examining the situations James addressed, we can get a good picture of what his readers were experiencing. Looking back at what you underlined in James 1, take a minute to list in the first column of the following chart anything James' readers appear to have been facing. You'll use the second column shortly.

James' Readers	Your Students

Based on what you've discovered in James 1, what do you think James' purpose was for writing this letter? What was he trying to get across to his readers?

Insight

Whom Was James Writing To?

Your students may wonder about James' reference to his readers: "To the twelve tribes scattered among the nations." Who were these people? The phrase *twelve tribes* refers to the Old Testament tribes of Israel. The phrase *scattered among the nations* comes from the Greek word *diaspora*, which described the Jewish people living outside of Palestine. However, there are several schools of thought concerning James' specific audience. Here are three possibilities:

- James was writing to Jewish Christians who lived outside of Palestine and were scattered because of persecution.
- James' intended audience was the true people of God—Jewish and Gentile believers—living in the last days.
- James was writing to all Christians who must now live in this physical world, separated from their true homeland in heaven.

In his letter, James makes several references that would have been familiar to Jewish Christians (James 1:23-25; 2:2, 8-13; 2:19; 4:11-12), indicating that may have been his audience. Other New Testament passages refer to this group in a similar way (for example, Acts 11:19). Plus, as you'll see in James' letter, he's a practical guy—not one to get too metaphorical. So the most literal option is probably the most accurate. The most likely conclusion is the first option: Jewish Christians who lived outside of Palestine.

Taking It Inward

Connecting Parallel Worlds

Looking back at the info you listed about James' readers, take a few minutes to draw some parallels between his audience and your students. What are some specific situations your students are facing that are comparable to what James' readers were facing? Write your thoughts in the second column of the chart above. Be sure to include the names of specific students when you describe the situations. In fact, take a minute to ask the Holy Spirit to bring to mind trials, temptations, and other challenges your students are facing.

Wrapping It Up

James: A Profile

Let's put it all together by reflecting on the faith journey of James, the brother of Jesus.

What are some reasons he was well suited to address these issues with the twelve tribes scattered among the nations?

Based on what you've observed in James 1, how would you describe James' concern for his readers?

What do you think motivated his concern?

How would you describe the relationship James had with his readers?

How does this relationship compare with the relationship you have with your students?

What are some ways you could be more of a James to your students?

WEB SUPPORT:
Don't forget to check out Web support for *Hear and Do* at www.inword.org. You'll find updated media suggestions such as music and video clips along with more prep helps and specific application ideas. Look for the Digging Deeper series icon. You'll find password information in the Instructions at the front of this book.

How can you encourage your students to be more of a James to the people around them?

What do you make of the fact that James didn't identify himself as Jesus' biological brother? (Talk about a way to have instant credibility!) Compare the claims he *could have made* to the way he presented himself in his letter.

Before wrapping up today's study, select the appropriate Teach It guide for your session. (Full Teach It guides are on the CD-ROM accompanying this book.) Then read through the guide so you're familiar with the flow of the session and confident with each exercise. Be sure to allow time for printing or photocopying the Scripture sheets and student journal pages, and pulling together any materials needed.

Before you close your book, spend some time praying for your students. Pray that God's Spirit will guide you in helping your students apply the truth explored in this session to the trials, temptations, and other challenges they are facing.

ONE WEEK OUT

Remind your students about the study and encourage them to come.

1. Materials

For this session each student will need—
- the James 1 Scripture sheet
- the student journal page for Session 1
- his or her own Bible and pen
- a notebook in which to keep all Scripture sheet and journal pages. (After this session have students insert the James 1 Scripture sheets and Session 1 journal page in the notebooks. Each week they'll add the new Scripture sheets and journal pages.)

You'll also need—
- a whiteboard and markers
- colored pencils (at least one color per student)
- a name placard for each James: James A, James B, and James C
- three chairs and a long table to set the stage for the game
- three copies of the James Name chart (see Open)
- optional: postage-paid postcards

2. Session Intro

GOALS OF SESSION 1

As students experience this session, they will—
- explore the many men named James in the New Testament and determine which James is the likely author.
- be introduced to the issues facing the first readers of the James letter.
- be challenged to be a James to people in their lives who are facing similar issues.

PRAYER

OPEN: *SETTING THE STAGE*
Group Interaction: Play a game similar to *To Tell the Truth*, asking questions to a panel of possible "Jameses," to discover which New Testament James wrote James.

3. Digging In: *Will the Real James Please Stand?*

Group Dig: Investigate info about several men named James mentioned in the New Testament.

4. Digging Deeper: *Being a Christian Wasn't Easy Then, Either*

Personal Retreat: Explore James 1 to see what James' readers were experiencing.

5. Wrapping It Up: *Pay It Forward*

Group Interaction: Challenge students to thank the Jameses in their lives, and to be a James in others' lives.

JAMES 1
THE JAMES GANG

ONE WEEK OUT

Remind your students about the study and encourage them to come.

1. Materials

For this session each student will need—
- the James 1 Scripture sheet
- the student journal page for Session 1
- his or her own Bible and pen
- a notebook in which to keep all Scripture sheet and journal pages. (After this session have students insert the James 1 Scripture sheets and Session 1 journal page in the notebooks. Each week they'll add the new Scripture sheets and journal pages.)

You'll also need—
- a whiteboard and markers
- colored pencils (at least one color per student)
- name placard for each James: James A, James B, and James C
- three chairs and a long table to set the stage for the game
- three copies of the James Name chart (see Open)
- optional: postage-paid postcards

2. Session Intro

GOALS OF SESSION 1

As students experience this session, they will—
- explore the many men named James in the New Testament and determine which James is the likely author.
- be introduced to the issues facing the first readers of James' letter.
- be challenged to be a James to people in their lives who are facing similar issues.

PRAYER

OPEN: *SETTING THE STAGE*

Group Interaction: Play a game similar to *To Tell the Truth* to discover which New Testament James wrote James.

3. Digging In: *Will the Real James Please Stand?*

Group Dig: Investigate info about several men named James mentioned in the New Testament in order to determine which James wrote James.

4. Digging Deeper: *Being a Christian Wasn't Easy Then, Either*

Personal Retreat: Explore James 1 to see what James' readers were experiencing.

5. Wrapping It Up: *Pay It Forward*

Group Interaction: Challenge students to thank the Jameses in their lives, and to be a James in others' lives.

ONE WEEK OUT

Remind your students about the study and encourage them to come.

1. Materials

For this session each student will need—
- the James 1 Scripture sheet
- the student journal page for Session 1
- his or her own Bible and pen
- a notebook in which to keep all Scripture sheet and journal pages. (After this session have students insert the James 1 Scripture sheets and Session 1 journal page in the notebooks. Each week they'll add the new Scripture sheets and journal pages.)

You'll also need—
- a whiteboard and markers
- colored pencils (at least one color per student)
- optional: postage-paid postcards

2. Session Intro

GOALS OF SESSION 1
As students experience this session, they will—
- explore the many men named James in the New Testament and determine which James is the likely author.
- be introduced to the issues facing the first readers of James' letter.
- be challenged to be a James to people in their lives who are facing similar issues.

PRAYER

OPEN: *SETTING THE STAGE*
Group Interaction: Do some quick brainstorming to gauge students' firsthand knowledge of the book of James.

3. Digging In: *Will the Real James Please Stand?*

Group Dig: Investigate info about several men named James mentioned in the New Testament in order to determine which James wrote James.

4. Digging Deeper: *Being a Christian Wasn't Easy Then, Either*

Personal Retreat: Explore James 1 to see what James' readers were experiencing.

5. Wrapping It Up: *Pay It Forward*

Group Interaction: Challenge students to thank the Jameses in their lives, and to be a James in others' lives.

ONE WEEK OUT

Remind your students about the study and encourage them to come.

1. Materials

For this session each student will need—
- the James 1 Scripture sheet
- the student journal page for Session 1
- his or her own Bible and pen
- a notebook in which to keep all Scripture sheet and journal pages. (After this session have students insert the James 1 Scripture sheets and Session 1 journal page in the notebooks. Each week they'll add the new Scripture sheets and journal pages.)

You'll also need—
- a whiteboard and markers
- colored pencils (at least one color per student)
- optional: postage-paid postcards

2. Session Intro

GOALS OF SESSION 1

As students experience this session, they will—
- explore the many men named James in the New Testament and determine which James is the likely author.
- be introduced to the issues facing the first readers of James' letter.
- be challenged to be a James to people in their lives who are facing similar issues.

PRAYER

OPEN: *SETTING THE STAGE*
Group Interaction: Do some quick brainstorming to gauge students' firsthand knowledge of the book of James.

3. Digging In: *Will the Real James Please Stand?*

Group Dig: Investigate info about several men named James mentioned in the New Testament in order to determine which James wrote James.

4. Cross-Checking: *Now That's a Conversion!*

Group Read: See what the sibling scene in John 7:1-7 adds to the mix.

5. Digging Deeper: *Being a Christian Wasn't Easy Then, Either*

Personal Retreat: Explore James 1 to see what James' readers were experiencing.

6. Wrapping It Up: *Pay It Forward*

Group Interaction: Challenge students to thank the Jameses in their lives, and to be a James in others' lives.

OUTLINE **COFFEEHOUSE** SESSION 1

ONE WEEK OUT

Challenge your gang to read James 1 before the first session.

You may want to send reminder notes, letting students know the time and place where the group will be meeting. Some coffeehouse chains (like Starbucks) have a "send an email invite to a friend" feature on their Web site; this may be fun to utilize. Remind your students to bring food and tip money, unless you're buying!

As you prepare for the first session, don't forget to allow time to gather any materials needed. (See the following Materials list.)

Most importantly, recruit a prayer team to pray specifically for this Bible study. Supply the team with helpful specifics, such as names of students, when you're meeting, and the subject matter you'll be covering.

1. Materials

For this session each student will need—
- his or her own Bible
- optional: journal page for Session 1 (Using the student journal page is optional in the coffeehouse setting because table space may be limited.)

You'll also need—
- stamped postcards
- a pack of pencils with erasers
- optional: a few spare Bibles for students who've forgotten theirs

2. Session Intro

GOALS OF SESSION 1
As students experience this session, they will—
- explore the many men named James in the New Testament and determine which James is the likely author.
- be introduced to the issues facing the first readers of James' letter.
- be challenged to be a James to people in their lives facing similar issues.

PRAYER

OPEN: *SETTING THE STAGE*

Group Interaction: Do some quick brainstorming to gauge students' firsthand knowledge of the book of James.

3. Digging In: *Will the Real James Please Stand?*

Group Dig: Investigate info about several men named James mentioned in the New Testament in order to determine which James wrote James.

4. Cross-Checking: *Now That's a Conversion!*

Group Read: See what the sibling scene in John 7:1-7 adds to the mix.

5. Digging Deeper: *Being a Christian Wasn't Easy Then, Either*

Group Dig: Explore James 1 to see what James' readers were experiencing.

6. Wrapping It Up: *Pay It Forward*

Group Interaction: Challenge students to thank the Jameses in their lives, and to be a James in others' lives.

1. Materials (Optional)

Video clip from the film *Remember the Titans:* Chapter 23, "Remember Forever"—DVD counter cues 1:18:00 to 1:20:04.

2. Optional Openings

Video clip: show a quick pep talk clip from *Remember the Titans*
Quotations: inspiring pep talk quotations

3. Digging In

Personal Story: Share a story that illustrates the value of perspective.

4. Digging Deeper

James 1:1-15

5. Taking It Inward

Who are the Jameses in your life and whom are you a James to?

6. Wrapping It Up

Challenge: Contact the Jameses in your life, and the people whom you might be a James to.

SESSION 2

Setting the Heart

No one—not God the Father, not Jesus, not the Holy Spirit—ever said the Christian life would be easy. In fact, the Bible tells us we can expect quite the opposite. As you prepare your heart to study James 1—a chapter warning us to expect trials—read some words from Jesus that give a heads-up on how to endure life's difficulties. Watch for what Jesus says to do and the payoff for doing it.

> Therefore everyone who hears these words of mine and puts them into practice is like a wise man who built his house on the rock. The rain came down, the streams rose, and the winds blew and beat against that house; yet it did not fall, because it had its foundation on the rock. But everyone who hears these words of mine and does not put them into practice is like a foolish man who built his house on sand. The rain came down, the streams rose, and the winds blew and beat against that house, and it fell with a great crash. (Matthew 7:24-27)

Digging In

What do you find here?

In Session 1 we glanced at the various situations addressed in James 1. You may have noticed that with each challenging situation, James provided some encouragement.

Read James 1:1-18 using your Scripture sheets, and circle any encouragement or instructions James gave concerning the situations below.

Then write this info in the right-hand column.

Problem	Encouragement/Instructions
trials (1:2)	

lack of wisdom (1:5)	
humble circumstances (1:9)	
temptation (1:13)	

Taking It Inward

You want me to do what?!

From the looks of it, things weren't going so well for James' readers. They were bombarded with trials, their circumstances were humble, and, to top it all, they were dogged by temptation. Sounds like a day in the life of a student—or even a youth leader—doesn't it?

So how about you? How have you been handling your trials, lack of wisdom, life circumstances, and temptations? Take a moment to put yourself in the place of James' readers.

In the first of the following sections (The Problem), write anything you're facing that parallels what James' audience must have been facing.

Then, based on James 1, in the second section write *how* you're instructed to respond to these problems. In the third section, write *why* you're encouraged to respond that way.

THE PROBLEM
What trials are you facing right now? (If life's great at the moment, answer this: What trials are you afraid to face?)

In what areas do you lack wisdom or feel deficient and inadequate?

How do you feel about your life status and circumstances?

What are your major areas of temptation? (Write in code if you prefer.)

THE RESPONSE
How do James' instructions help you respond to these problems?

1.

2.

3.

4.

THE REASON
Read James 1 carefully, and you'll find at least one reason why you should respond this way.

1.

2.

3.

4.

Digging Deeper

Make It Personal

There's a good chance that you identify with one of the situations in James' letter more than the others. Scripture is packed with teaching and encouragement for all four situations, but for the next exercise, choose the one or two that resonate most with you. (If you have extra time, feel free to take a look at all four.)

With each situation, you'll be asked what you can change—right now—to respond to it the way the Lord asks you to. Here are some guidelines to use in responding:

- Be specific. Write down specific actions you can do within the next 24 hours.
- Be prayerful. Ask the Holy Spirit what he's eager to say to you on this subject.
- Be intentional. Don't gloss over this exercise. Use it as an opportunity to show God that you're serious about obeying his Word.

TRIALS

As you read the following passages, look for answers to these questions:

- What kinds of trials are described?
- What are the rewards for standing firm?
- What encouragement is given?

Matthew 5:10-12

John 16:33

2 Corinthians 1:3-7

Hebrews 10:32-39

1 Peter 1:6-9

The verses you just read are packed with rewards for those who stand firm through the rough stuff. How can these rewards motivate you to "consider it pure joy" when you face trials of many kinds?

LACKING WISDOM

As you read the next three passages, look for the following information:

- What is the context of the passage?
- What do you learn about God?
- What parallels do you see between this situation and James 1?

1 Kings 3:6-14

Daniel 1:17-21

Daniel 2:19-23

What changes do you need to make in order to receive wisdom as Solomon and Daniel did?

HUMBLE CIRCUMSTANCES

As you read the next four passages, write down what God's people are to focus on.

Matthew 23:11-12

Philippians 4:11-13

1 Timothy 6:7-11

Hebrews 13:5-6

What adjustments do you need to make in order to pursue the things of God (which may lead to humble circumstances) rather than the things of the world (which may lead to comfortable—even luxurious—circumstances)?

TEMPTATION

As you read the following passages, look for the answers to these questions:

- What's the root of temptation?
- What are the consequences of caving in to temptation?
- What can give you strength to beat temptation?

Genesis 3:1-7

2 Corinthians 12:7-10

Hebrews 2:17-3:1

James 1:13-15

Write down three observations from these verses—things to do or ways to think—that can help you conquer temptation.

1.

2.

3.

Wrapping It Up

You too can keep from falling!

Do you have issues? Fortunately, God doesn't leave us to our own devices as we navigate the challenges life throws our way. In fact, if we'd just follow the instructions James gives and trust the encouragement he offers, we'd be like the wise man Jesus described in Matthew 7. And we wouldn't fall.

Before wrapping up today's study, select the appropriate Teach It guide for your session. (Full Teach It guides are on the CD-ROM accompanying this book.) Then read through the guide so you're familiar with the flow of the session and confident with each exercise. Be sure to allow time for printing or photocopying the Scripture sheets and student journal pages, and pulling together any materials needed.

Before you close your book, take a moment to think about your students and how their lives might parallel the lives of James' readers: facing trials, lacking wisdom, living meagerly, beating temptation. Pray that your students will be able to clearly see in their lives the responses and solutions that James offers.

EXERCISE HEADS-UP
High School 1 Session 4 contains a Large-Group Option (for the opening) that involves collecting video interviews before the session. You may want to take a look at that now.

WEB SUPPORT:
Don't forget to check out Web support for *Hear and Do* at www.inword.org. You'll find updated media suggestions such as music and video clips along with more prep helps and specific application ideas. Look for the Digging Deeper series icon. You'll find password information in the Instructions at the front of this book.

1. Materials

For this session each student will need—
- the James 1 Scripture sheet
- the student journal page for Session 2
- his or her own Bible, pen, and notebook

You'll also need—
- a whiteboard and markers
- colored pencils (at least two colors per student)
- a video clip from the movie *Millions:* Chapter 4, "Real Money"—DVD counter cues 00:15:46 to 00:18:52
- address labels (see Taking It Inward)
- a box of objects or folder of pictures representing various issues in James: Fishing lure (remove the hook for safety), plastic handcuffs, tall stool, footstool or toddler chair, picture of a question mark or ocean waves, empty wallet or an old, worn-out shoe, wad of play money, butterfly, ruler or report card, dictionary for Taking it Inward
- tape

2. Session Intro

GOALS OF SESSION 2
As students experience this session, they will—
- explore the problems faced by the first readers of James.
- discover how James' instructions and encouragement on these issues can help us today.
- examine their personal struggles and apply the encouragement from James.

OPEN: *ISSUE INTRO*
Group Share: What would you do with $5 million?
Video Clip: *Million*

3. Digging In: *What Do You Find Here?*

Group Dig: Explore James 1:1-18 to discover instructions and encouragement for facing some hard life issues.

4. Digging Deeper: *Make It Personal—Build Your Own*

Personal Retreat: Students can customize the study with a build-your-own exercise in a related Scripture passage.

5. Taking It Inward: *Taking It to Heart*

Group Interaction: Process the life issues in James with a hands-on matching exercise.

6. Wrapping It Up: *You Too Can Keep from Falling!*

Group Prayer: Students pray about the issues they're facing.

JAMES 1:1-18
DO YOU HAVE ISSUES?

1. Materials

For this session each student will need—
- the James 1 Scripture sheet
- the student journal page for Session 2
- his or her own Bible, pen, and notebook

You'll also need—
- a whiteboard and markers
- colored pencils (at least two colors per student)
- optional: C-clamp or Vise-Grip pliers, a dictionary, a penny or an empty wallet, a fishing lure
- Large-Group Option: images to project of C-clamp or Vise-Grip pliers, a dictionary, a penny or an empty wallet, a fishing lure

2. Session Intro

GOALS OF SESSION 2

As students experience this session, they will—
- explore the problems faced by the first readers of James.
- discover how James' instructions and encouragement on these issues can help us today.
- examine their personal struggles and apply the encouragement from James.

PRAYER

OPEN: *ISSUE INTRO*
Brainstorm Discussion: What are the deepest issues facing teenagers today?

3. Digging In: *What Do You Find Here?*

Group Dig: Explore James 1:1-18 to discover instructions and encouragement for facing some hard life issues.

4. Digging Deeper: *Make It Personal—Build Your Own*

Personal Retreat: Students can customize the study with a build-your-own exercise in a related Scripture passage.
Large-Group Option: Students will work in small groups to address one of the issues in James.

5. Taking It Inward: *Taking It to Heart*

Group Share: Students help one other apply James' instructions and encouragement to personal issues they are facing. (Optional: use items that represent each issue.)
Large-Group Option: Each small group teaches the others about the issue they studied.

6. Wrapping It Up: *You Too Can Keep from Falling*

Group Prayer: Students pray about the issues they're facing.

1. Materials

For this session each student will need—
- the James 1 Scripture sheet
- the student journal page for Session 2
- his or her own Bible, pen, and notebook

You'll also need—
- a whiteboard and markers
- colored pencils (at least two colors per student)
- optional: C-clamp or Vise-Grip pliers, a dictionary, a penny or an empty wallet, a fishing lure

2. Session Intro

GOALS OF SESSION 2
As students experience this session, they will—
- explore the problems faced by the first readers of James.
- discover how James' instructions and encouragement on these issues can help us today.
- examine their personal struggles and apply the encouragement from James.

PRAYER

OPEN: *ISSUE INTRO*
Brainstorm Discussion: What are the deepest issues facing teenagers today?

3. Digging In: *What Do You Find Here?*

Group Dig: Explore James 1:1-18 to discover instructions and encouragement for dealing with some hard life issues.

4. Digging Deeper: *Make It Personal—Build Your Own*

Personal Retreat: Students can customize the study with a build-your-own exercise that takes a detailed look at the issues.

5. Taking It Inward: *Taking It to Heart*

Group Share: Students help each other apply James' instructions and encouragement to personal issues.

6. Wrapping It Up: *You Too Can Keep from Falling*

Group Prayer: Students pray with each other about the issues they're facing.

1. Materials

For this session each student will need—
- the James 1 Scripture sheet
- the student journal page for Session 2
- his or her own Bible, pen, and notebook

You'll also need—
- a whiteboard and markers
- colored pencils (at least two colors per student)
- the promo movie trailer for *The Lord of the Rings: The Fellowship of the Ring*, from the special features DVD that accompanies the movie. (At its Main Menu, click Theatrical Trailers, then click Final Trailer. You may also be able to find this trailer online.)
- black-and-white pictures representing life issues (see Taking It Inward)
- any available camera phones from students

2. Session Intro

GOALS OF SESSION 2
As students experience this session, they will—
- explore the problems faced by the first readers of James.
- discover how James' instructions and encouragement on these issues can help us today.
- examine their personal struggles and apply the encouragement from James.

PRAYER

OPEN: *ISSUE INTRO*
Brainstorm Discussion: Compare the issues in James to those faced by key characters in *The Lord of the Rings: The Fellowship of the Ring.*

3. Digging In: *What Do You Find Here?*

Group Dig: Explore James 1:1-18 to discover instructions and encouragement for dealing with some hard life issues.

4. Digging Deeper: *Make It Personal—Build Your Own*

Personal Retreat: Students can customize the study with a build-your-own exercise in several related Scripture passages.

5. Taking It Inward: *Taking It to Heart*

Group Share: Use photos and images that depict life issues to help one another apply the instructions and encouragement from James.

6. Wrapping It Up: *You Too Can Keep from Falling*

Pray with a partner and create visual reminders (using available camera phones) to help students continue praying throughout the week.

1. Materials

For this session each student will need—
- his or her own Bible
- optional: journal page for Session 2 (Using the student journal page is optional in the coffeehouse setting because table space may be limited.)

You'll also need—
- a pack of pencils with erasers
- optional: a few spare Bibles for students who've forgotten theirs

2. Session Intro

GOALS OF SESSION 2

As students experience this session, they will—
- explore the problems faced by the first readers of James.
- discover how James' instructions and encouragement on these issues can help us today.
- examine their personal struggles and apply the encouragement from James.

PRAYER

OPEN: *ISSUE INTRO*
People Watch: Speculate on issues people might be facing.

3. Digging In: *What Do You Find Here?*

Personal Study: Explore James 1:1-18 to discover instructions and encouragement for dealing with hard life issues.

4. Taking It Inward: *Taking It to Heart*

Group Share: Students apply James' instructions and encouragement to the issues they personally face.

5. Wrapping It Up: *You Too Can Keep from Falling*

Group Prayer: Students pray about the issues they're facing.

1. Materials (Optional)
- Video clip from the film *Groundhog Day*: Chapter 8-10, "Groundhog Day 3," "Gobbler's Knob 3," "Phil Seeks Help"—DVD counter cues 00:26:05-00:28:27
- Kite string or dental floss

2. Optional Openings

Video Clip: *Groundhog Day*
Visual Illustration: Use a kite string as a time line representing eternity
Quotations: The value of overcoming adversity and opposition
Personal Story: How trials or struggles give us something we need

3. Digging In

James 1:2-8
Personal Story: Enjoying the rewards of beating adversity
God's Perspective: He sees how our adversity fits into the big picture
Our Perspective: It would be nice if life were easy, but…

4. Taking It Inward

God wants to give us what we need to overcome, without finding fault. We need to boldly ask, without doubting him.

5. Wrapping It Up

A challenge to pray Plan A!

SESSION 3

Setting the Heart

God has always been generous with people who are obedient. From Day One (actually from Day Six, beginning with the creation of man), God has placed a premium on obedience. We're all required to know God's commands, but heeding them seems to come with a special set of promises. As you prepare to study James again, read Deuteronomy 6:1-3. These are the words of Moses, spoken as he prepared God's people to take possession of the Promised Land. Notice the emphasis on heeding God's decrees and the payoff for doing so.

> These are the commands, decrees and laws the LORD your God directed me to teach you to observe in the land that you are crossing the Jordan to possess, so that you, your children and their children after them may fear the LORD your God as long as you live by keeping all his decrees and commands that I give you, and so that you may enjoy long life. Hear, O Israel, and be careful to obey so that it may go well with you and that you may increase greatly in a land flowing with milk and honey, just as the LORD, the God of your fathers, promised you. (Deuteronomy 6:1-3)

Digging In

Read Instructions before Engaging Life

Begin by reading James 1:19-27 from your Scripture sheets. As you read, mark every instruction James gives his readers.

Then look back at what you marked, and list the instructions in this passage.

Read the passage a second time and write in the following space anything these verses teach us about God.

Taking It Inward

Finally, a Reason to Stop Praying (About One Thing, at Least)

How many times have you asked God about his will for your life? Have you ever realized God has already told you what his will is? In just these nine verses, we are given guidelines concerning our inner and outer behavior—behavior that God desires and accepts. Perhaps doing God's will is simpler than we think.

For the next few minutes, think about a 60-day stretch in your life—the past 30 days and the next 30 days. Rate yourself on how well you've obeyed each of these instructions over the past 30 days. If God's Spirit brings to mind specific situations when you blew it, write them down.

Instructions	Past 30 Days	Next 30 Days
Be quick to listen, slow to speak (1:19)		
Be slow to become angry (1:19)		
Get rid of all moral filth and evil (1:21)		
Humbly accept the word planted in you (1:21)		
Do what the Word says (1:22)		
Keep a tight rein on your tongue (1:26)		

Look after orphans and widows in distress (1:27)		
Keep from being polluted by the world (1:27)		

Now for the challenge. What can you do over the next 30 days to better obey these instructions? Try to respond with specific examples. For instance, next to the instruction to look after widows and orphans, write down specific names, along with tasks you can do in the coming month. (For example, "Rake Mrs. Adams' leaves.")

We're given a promise in James 1:25—something we're guaranteed if we follow the perfect law. Write that promise in the space that follows.

Cross-Checking

Hear, Then Do

James 1:25 emphasizes a pattern that shows up throughout the entire Bible—first hear, then do the Word. It's a pattern that figures prominently in Jesus' teaching. If the tight relationship between hearing and doing hasn't sunk in yet (or even if it has), read the words of Jesus in each of the following verses. Be sure to note the context of each passage. Then write down the phrases Jesus used for hearing and doing, along with any promises you can enjoy when you hear and do the Word of God.

Matthew 7:24-25

Luke 11:28

John 14:21

Digging Deeper

The Deceit Factor

James warns us of two ways we can deceive ourselves. Find these warnings in James 1:19-27, and write them here.

Could you be deceived in these areas? The problem with self-deception is that if we're deceiving ourselves, we may not even know it! Take a couple of minutes to assess your self-deception level by prayerfully responding to the following warnings and questions.

WARNING 1: DON'T MERELY LISTEN TO THE WORD; DO WHAT IT SAYS.

Think about your activities over the past 10 days. Is your agenda the same as God's? If not, whose agenda have you been following—yours or God's?

How often does your personal Bible study lead to action—a significant response to your study?

Think about the last time you were motivated or challenged by a Christian speaker or teacher. About how long ago was that? What actions resulted from that motivation once you got home?

Consider the prevalence of Christian television, music, magazines, books, and conferences today—and the number of believers who "hear the Word" through these media. Is the gospel penetrating our culture as a result of all the church is hearing? Compare what you see in the church at large with what you read in James 1:22-25.

WARNING 2: KEEP A TIGHT REIN ON YOUR TONGUE.
The phrase *tight rein* probably relates to James' earlier reference to being slow to speak (1:19). We'll be looking at the devastating effects of gossip later in our study of James.

Picture the last time someone complained to you about something you did, such as a decision you made or a plan you implemented. Were you slow to speak and quick to listen?

When you're in a position to defend your opinion, can you describe yourself as having a tight rein on your tongue? Does the need to win override the Bible's command to control what you say?

Wrapping It Up

So Act Already!

Wherever God has spoken to your heart—impressed an idea into your mind—is where you need to apply what you've uncovered in James 1. If you need some suggestions for doing the instructions from this section of James, read over the Wrapping It Up exercise in Teach It. Then take some action! Perhaps you need to pick up the phone and call a widow you know. Maybe you need to apologize to someone for being quick to speak and slow to listen.

But here's a word of warning: Don't do the Word simply to set an example for your students. That's noble, but it's not authentic. Do the Word out of obedience to what God has put on your heart. In fact, don't finish this study time until God's Spirit has led you to a specific action. Then do it!

Before wrapping up today's study, select the appropriate Teach It guide for your session. (Full Teach It guides are on the CD-ROM accompanying this book.) Then read through the guide so you're familiar with the flow of the session and confident with each exercise. Be sure to allow time for printing or photocopying the Scripture sheets and student journal pages, and pulling together any materials needed.

As you finish your prep time, take a few minutes to pray for your students. Pray that their hearts will be open to what God wants them to hear from James, and then be willing to act on it.

WEB SUPPORT:
Don't forget to check out Web support for *Hear and Do* at www.inword.org. You'll find updated media suggestions such as music and video clips along with more prep helps and specific application ideas. Look for the Digging Deeper series icon. You'll find password information in the Instructions at the front of this book.

EXERCISE HEADS-UP

High School 1 Session 4 contains a Large-Group Option (for the opening) that involves collecting video interviews before the session. If you haven't already, you may want to take a look at that now.

1. Materials

For this session each student will need—
- the James 1 Scripture sheet
- the student journal page for Session 3
- his or her own Bible, pen, and notebook

You'll also need—
- a whiteboard and markers
- colored pencils (at least two colors per student)
- two signs, one that reads "You Are Here" and one that reads "God's Will"
- optional: your church directory or local phone book

2. Session Intro

GOALS OF SESSION 3

As students experience this session, they will—
- discover the detailed instructions James gives for living out the Christian faith.
- explore what these instructions teach us about God and obedience.
- be challenged to use these detailed instructions as a gateway for discovering what God wants them to do.

PRAYER

OPEN: *GOD'S WILL PRIMER*
Group Interaction: Play a game similar to *Mother, May I,* to illustrate the dynamics of finding God's will.

3. Digging In: *Read Instructions before Engaging Life*

Group Dig: Explore James 1:19-27 to learn key info about God and James' readers.

4. Taking It Inward: *From the Inside Out*

Group Interaction: Determine which instructions from God in James are for our inner selves and which are for our outer selves.

5. Digging Deeper: *Hear, Then Do*

Group Solitude: Interact with God about the connection between hearing and doing his words.

6. Taking It Inward: *So Act Already!*

Group Interaction: Develop a strategy for cranking up the intensity on hearing and doing the Word of God.

7. Wrapping It Up: *Start Simple*

Group Interaction: Finding and doing God's will is simpler than we think.

1. Materials

For this session each student will need—
- the James 1 Scripture sheet
- the student journal page for Session 3
- his or her own Bible, pen, and notebook

You'll also need—
- a whiteboard and markers
- colored pencils (at least two colors per student)
- optional: your church directory or local phone book

2. Session Intro

GOALS OF SESSION 3

As students experience this session, they will—
- discover the detailed instructions James gives for living out the Christian faith.
- explore what these instructions teach us about God and obedience.
- be challenged to use these detailed instructions as a gateway for discovering what God wants them to do.

PRAYER

OPEN: *GOD'S WILL PRIMER*
Group Interaction: Brainstorm ways we try to discover God's will.

3. Digging In: *Read Instructions before Engaging Life*

Group Dig: Explore James 1:19-27 to learn key info about God and James' readers.

4. Taking It Inward: *From the Inside Out*

Group Interaction: Determine which instructions from God in James are for our inner life and which are for our outer life.

5. Cross-Checking: *Hear, Then Do*

Small-Group Dig: Explore the Gospels to see what Jesus had to say on the subject of *hear and do.*

6. Digging Deeper: *Doing the Two-Step*

Personal Retreat: Interact with God about the connection between hearing and doing his Word.

7. Taking It Inward: *So Act Already!*

Group Interaction: Develop a strategy for cranking up the intensity on hearing and doing the Word of God.

8. Wrapping It Up: *Start Simple*

Group Interaction: Finding and doing God's will is simpler than we think.

JAMES 1:19-27
KEEP IT SIMPLE

1. Materials

For this session each student will need—
- The James 1 Scripture sheet
- the student journal page for Session 3
- his or her own Bible, pen, and notebook

You'll also need—
- a whiteboard and markers
- colored pencils (at least two colors per student)
- optional: your church directory or local phone book

2. Session Intro

GOALS OF SESSION 3

As students experience this session, they will—
- discover the detailed instructions James gives for living out the Christian faith.
- explore what these instructions teach us about God and about obedience.
- be challenged to use these detailed instructions as a gateway for discovering what God wants them to do.

PRAYER

OPEN: *GOD'S WILL PRIMER*
Group Interaction: Brainstorm ways we try to discover God's will.

3. Digging In: *Read Instructions before Engaging Life*

Group Dig: Explore James 1:19-27 to learn key info about God and James' readers.

4. Taking It Inward: *From the Inside Out*

Group Interaction: Determine which instructions from God in James are for our inner life and which are for our outer life.

5. Digging Deeper: *Hear, Then Do*

Personal Retreat: Explore the Gospels to see what Jesus had to say on the subject of *hear and do*.

6. Taking It Inward: *So Act Already!*

Group Interaction: Develop a strategy for cranking up the intensity on hearing and doing the Word of God.

7. Wrapping It Up: *Start Simple*

Group Interaction: Finding and doing God's will is simpler than we think.

1. Materials

For this session each student will need—
- the James 1 Scripture sheet
- the student journal page for Session 3
- his or her own Bible, pen, and notebook

You'll also need—
- a whiteboard and markers
- colored pencils (at least two colors per student)
- optional: your church directory or local phone book

2. Session Intro

GOALS OF SESSION 3

As students experience this session, they will—
- discover the detailed instructions James gives for living out the Christian faith.
- explore what these instructions teach us about God and about obedience.
- be challenged to use these detailed instructions as a gateway for discovering what God wants them to do.

PRAYER

OPEN: *GOD'S WILL PRIMER*
Group Interaction: Brainstorm ways we try to discover God's will.

3. Digging In: *Read Instructions before Engaging Life*

Group Dig: Explore James 1:19-27 to learn key info about God and James' readers.

4. Taking It Inward: *From the Inside Out*

Group Interaction: Determine which instructions from God in James are for our inner life and which are for our outer life.

5. Digging Deeper: *Hear, Then Do*

Personal Retreat: Explore the Gospels to see what Jesus had to say on the subject of *hear and do.*

6. Taking It Inward: *So Act Already!*

Group Interaction: Develop a super-specific strategy for cranking up the intensity on hearing and doing the Word of God.

7. Wrapping It Up: *Start Simple*

Group Interaction: Finding and doing God's will is simpler than we think.

1. Materials

For this session each student will need—
- his or her own Bible and pen
- optional: journal page for Session 3 (Using the student journal page is optional in the coffeehouse setting because table space may be limited.)

You'll also need—
- a pack of pencils with erasers
- optional: a few spare Bibles for students who've forgotten theirs
- optional: your church directory or local phone book
- eight to 10 napkins you can write on

2. Session Intro

GOALS OF SESSION 3

As students experience this session, they will—
- discover the detailed instructions James gives for living out the Christian faith.
- explore what these instructions teach us about God and obedience.
- be challenged to use these detailed instructions as a gateway for discovering what God wants them to do.

PRAYER

OPEN: *GOD'S WILL PRIMER*
Group Interaction: Brainstorm ways we try to discover God's will.

3. Digging In: *Read Instructions before Engaging Life*

Group Dig: Explore James 1:19-27 to learn key info about God and James' readers.

4. Taking It Inward: *From the Inside Out*

Group Interaction: Determine which instructions from God in James are for our inner life and which are for our outer life.

5. Digging Deeper: *Hear, Then Do*

Group Dig: Explore the Gospels to see what Jesus had to say on the subject of *hear and do*.

6. Taking It Inward: *So Act Already!*

Group Interaction: Develop a super-specific strategy for cranking up the intensity on hearing and doing the Word of God.

7. Wrapping It Up: *Start Simple*

Group Interaction: Finding and doing God's will is simpler than we think.

1. Materials (Optional)

- A promo video from a child sponsorship or humanitarian relief organization
- Images from a child sponsorship or relief organization

2. Optional Openings

Video Clip: Open with a promo video from a child sponsorship or humanitarian relief organization.

Visual Illustration: roll a media presentation showing images from various child sponsorship or relief organizations.

Quotations: Share quotations that were written or spoken to inspire action.

3. Digging In

Personal Story: Share a personal story about a time when you were inspired to action.

4. Digging Deeper

James 1:27

5. Wrapping It Up

Challenge: Picture what each of James' instructions can look like in your world.

SESSION 4

Setting the Heart

Congratulations! As you finish today's session prep, you're one-third of the way through this study in James. In the last three weeks as you've thoroughly studied the first chapter of James' letter, it's quite possible you've been spending more time than usual in God's Word. As you've studied, have you noticed an elevated desire to know and obey God? The real purpose of an in-depth Bible study isn't simply to know more about the book, but to know God himself. As we know God, our desire to obey him—follow him wholeheartedly—naturally increases.

You've probably noticed that James doesn't leave much room for guesswork on how we are to obey God. As you prepare for today's study in James 2, take a moment to hear what the apostle Peter—a guy who knew a lot about obedience—had to say about letting the Word change your behavior.

> Now that you have purified yourselves by obeying the truth so that you have sincere love for your brothers, love one another deeply, from the heart. For you have been born again, not of perishable seed, but of imperishable, through the living and enduring word of God. For, "All men are like grass, and all their glory is like the flowers of the field; the grass withers and the flowers fall, but the word of the Lord stands forever." And this is the word that was preached to you. (1 Peter 1:22-25)

Digging In

Favoritism 101

Read James 2:1-13 from your Scripture sheet. As you read, mark each of the following with a unique symbol or color:

- references to favoritism, the poor, and the rich
- references to the readers of James' letter
- references to God

Now take a moment to process what you've read by answering a few classic *who, what, when, where, why,* and *how* type questions.

What instructions does James give his readers?

What do you learn about favoritism?

What do you learn about God?

What conclusions can you draw about the situation of the recipients of James' letter?

How are the recipients described?

What's been done to or for them?

What have they been doing that runs counter to God's desires?

How are they like you?

How are they like the students in your ministry?

Taking It Inward

The Poor—Near and Dear to God's Heart

The message of the gospel is the great socioeconomic equalizer. The external stuff—clothes, salary, house, car—really doesn't matter. God sees nothing but the heart when he's dishing out grace and mercy. When we're carrying out the ministry of the gospel, he asks us to look at the same thing. Our tendency, however, is to focus on externals and gravitate toward those who are most like us—which is the first step in showing favoritism.

The significance of this next exercise is huge. To guarantee that you don't rush it, grab a glass of your favorite beverage and spend some time letting the Lord speak to your heart about one of his favorite subjects: the poor. As you read each of the following passages, jot down anything you learn about ministering to the poor.

WHAT GOD SAYS ON THE SUBJECT
    Leviticus 19:15

    Deuteronomy 15:7-11

    Zechariah 7:8-12

WHAT JESUS SAYS ON THE SUBJECT
    Luke 4:18-19

    Luke 12:29-34

    Luke 14:12-14

WHAT THE FIRST CHRISTIANS SAY ON THE SUBJECT
    Acts 10:1-2

    Acts 24:17

    Romans 15:25-26

    Galatians 2:9-10

What conclusions are you coming to concerning the priority of ministering to the poor?

How do your priorities compare with God's priorities?

Taking It Inward

Of Course You Don't Discriminate...or Do You?

Consider the following take on James 2:2-4:

You're hosting an outreach event in order to launch an evangelism effort at the local high school. Through the door walks a student who's the son of a prominent family in your community and a favorite among the faculty and students. Behind him is a teen who's introverted and quiet. This student is actually disliked at the school because he's unmotivated and disrespectful. If you make every effort to establish a relationship with the first student and hope that your volunteers make contact with the second student, have you discriminated among the students and become a judge with evil thoughts?

Well, have you? Take a moment to reflect on any situations in which you've operated with even a hint of the discrimination James describes. In the space that follows, write what comes to mind.

Think about the poor who are involved in your student ministry. (You may need to broaden your definition of the poor to include those who are poor in social skills, leadership abilities, intellect, athletic abilities, or interpersonal relationships.) Have you ever, even momentarily, looked at such a student and thought, *This isn't somebody I can build a program around*?

If you spend time on a school campus connecting with students, consider that setting for a moment. With whom do you seek to build relationships? Is it with student leaders? Popular kids? Athletes?

What is God saying to you about the poor around you?

WEB SUPPORT:
Don't forget to check out Web support for *Hear and Do* at www.inword.org. You'll find updated media suggestions such as music and video clips along with more prep helps and specific application ideas. Look for the Digging Deeper series icon. You'll find password information in the Instructions at the front of this book.

What is he prompting you to do regarding the poor in your student ministry?

Wrapping It Up

Thus Saith the Lord: No Cliques!

Before wrapping up today's study, select the appropriate Teach It guide for your session. (Full Teach It guides are on the CD-ROM accompanying this book.) Then read through the guide so you're familiar with the flow of the group session and confident with each exercise. Be sure to allow time for printing or photocopying the Scripture sheets and student journal pages, and pulling together any materials needed.

Finish your prep time by praying for your students—that their hearts will begin to break for the same things that break God's heart. Heartbreak for the poor is a good place to start.

EXERCISE HEADS-UP
High School 1 Session 4 contains a Large-Group Option (for the opening) that involves collecting video interviews before the session. This will take some additional prep.

1. Materials

For this session each student will need—
- the James 2 Scripture sheet
- the student journal page for Session 4
- his or her own Bible, pen, and notebook

You'll also need—
- a whiteboard and markers
- colored pencils (at least three colors per student)

2. Session Intro

GOALS OF SESSION 4

As students experience this session, they will—
- discover how much God despises favoritism.
- evaluate whether favoritism of any kind has crept into their lives.
- put specific steps in motion that will help your student ministry not only avoid favoritism but be a place of affirmation for all.

PRAYER

OPEN: *PERSONAL FAVES*

Group Interaction: Lead your group in a brainstorm discussion of their favorite things, from favorite superheroes to favorite days of the week.

3. Digging In: *Favoritism 101*

Group Dig: Explore James 2:1-13 to find out how the original readers of James were showing favoritism.

4. Taking It Inward: *Of Course You Don't Discriminate...or Do You?*

Group Interaction: Showing favoritism may be more prevalent and sinister than we think.

5. Digging Deeper: *The Poor—Near and Dear to God's Heart*

Personal Retreat: An opportunity for students to hear what weighs heavy on God's heart.

6. Taking It Inward: *The Futility of Favoritism*

Group Interaction: An opportunity for students to compare their hearts with God's heart.

7. Wrapping It Up: *Thus Saith the Lord: "No Cliques!"*

Group Interaction: A work session to put safeguards in place to eliminate favoritism.

JAMES 2:1-13
NOTHIN' BUT HEART

1. Materials

For this session each student will need—
- the James 2 Scripture sheet
- the student journal page for Session 4
- his or her own Bible, pen, and notebook

You'll also need—
- a whiteboard and markers
- colored pencils (at least three colors per student)
- optional: video interviews of students sharing their favorite things

2. Session Intro

GOALS OF SESSION 4

As students experience this session, they will—
- discover how much God despises favoritism.
- evaluate whether favoritism of any kind has crept into their lives.
- put specific steps in motion to help your student ministry not only avoid favoritism, but be a place of affirmation for all.

PRAYER

OPEN: *PERSONAL FAVES*
Group Interaction: Lead your group in a brainstorm discussion of their favorite things.

Large-Group Option: Show video interviews of students sharing their favorite things.

3. Digging In: *Favoritism 101*

Group Dig: Explore James 2:1-13 to find out how the original readers of James were showing favoritism.

4. Taking It Inward: *Of Course You Don't Discriminate...or Do You?*

Group Interaction: Showing favoritism may be more prevalent and sinister than we think.

5. Digging Deeper: *The Poor—Near and Dear to God's Heart*

Small-Group Dig: An opportunity for students to read about what weighs heavy on God's heart.

6. Taking It Inward: *The Futility of Favoritism*

Group Interaction: An opportunity for students to compare their hearts with God's heart.

7. Wrapping It Up: *Thus Saith the Lord: "No Cliques!"*

Group Interaction: A work session to put safeguards in place to eliminate favoritism.

JAMES 2:1-13
NOTHIN' BUT HEART

1. Materials

For this session each student will need—
- the James 2 Scripture sheet
- the student journal page for Session 4
- his or her own Bible, pen, and notebook

You'll also need—
- a whiteboard and markers
- colored pencils (at least three colors per student)

2. Session Intro

GOALS OF SESSION 4

As students experience this session, they will—
- discover how much God despises favoritism.
- evaluate whether favoritism of any kind has crept into their lives.
- put specific steps in motion to help your student ministry not only avoid favoritism, but be a place of affirmation for all.

PRAYER

OPEN: *PERSONAL FAVES*

Group Interaction: Lead your group in a brainstorm discussion of their favorite things.

3. Digging In: *Favoritism 101*

Group Dig: Explore James 2:1-13 to find out how the original readers of James were showing favoritism.

4. Taking It Inward: *Of Course You Don't Discriminate...or Do You?*

Group Interaction: Showing favoritism may be more prevalent and sinister than we think.

5. Digging Deeper: *The Poor—Near and Dear to God's Heart*

Personal Retreat: An opportunity for students to read about what weighs heavy on God's heart.

6. Taking It Inward: *The Futility of Favoritism*

Group Interaction: An opportunity for students to compare their hearts with God's heart.

7. Wrapping It Up: *Thus Saith the Lord: "No Cliques!"*

Group Interaction: A work session to put safeguards in place to eliminate favoritism.

OUTLINE **COLLEGE AGE** SESSION 4

1. Materials

For this session each student will need—
- the James 2 Scripture sheet
- the student journal page for Session 4
- his or her own Bible, pen, and notebook

You'll also need—
- a whiteboard and markers
- colored pencils (at least three colors per student)

2. Session Intro

GOALS OF SESSION 4

As students experience this session, they will—
- discover how much God despises favoritism.
- evaluate whether favoritism of any kind has crept into their lives.
- put specific steps in motion to help your student ministry not only avoid favoritism, but be a place of affirmation for all.

PRAYER

OPEN: *PERSONAL FAVES*

Group Interaction: Lead your group in a brainstorm discussion of their favorite things.

3. Digging In: *Favoritism 101*

Group Dig: Explore James 2:1-13 to find out how the original readers of James were showing favoritism.

4. Taking It Inward: *Of Course You Don't Discriminate...or Do You?*

Group Interaction: Showing favoritism may be more prevalent and sinister than we think.

5. Digging Deeper: *The Poor—Near and Dear to God's Heart*

Personal Retreat: An opportunity for students to read about what weighs heavy on God's heart.

6. Taking It Inward: *The Futility of Favoritism*

Group Interaction: An opportunity for students to compare their hearts with God's heart.

7. Wrapping It Up: *Thus Saith the Lord: "No Favoritism!"*

Group Interaction: A work session to put safeguards in place to eliminate favoritism.

1. Materials

For this session each student will need—
- his or her own Bible and pen
- optional: journal page for Session 4 (Using the student journal pages is optional in the coffeehouse setting because table space may be limited.)

You'll also need—
- a pack of pencils with erasers
- optional: a few spare Bibles for students who've forgotten theirs

2. Session Intro

GOALS OF SESSION 4

As students experience this session, they will—
- discover how much God despises favoritism.
- evaluate whether favoritism of any kind has crept into their lives.
- put specific steps in motion to help your student ministry not only avoid favoritism, but be a place of affirmation for all.

PRAYER

OPEN: *PERSONAL FAVES*

Group Interaction: Lead your group in a brainstorm discussion of their favorite things, from their favorite color to their favorite coffeehouse drink.

3. Digging In: *Favoritism 101*

Group Dig: Explore James 2:1-13 to find out how the original readers of James were showing favoritism.

4. Taking It Inward: *Of Course You Don't Discriminate...or Do You?*

Group Interaction: Showing favoritism may be more prevalent and sinister than we think.

5. Digging Deeper: *The Poor—Near and Dear to God's Heart*

Personal Retreat: An opportunity for students to hear what weighs heavy on God's heart.

6. Taking It Inward: *The Futility of Favoritism*

Group Interaction: An opportunity for students to compare their hearts with God's heart.

7. Wrapping It Up: *Thus Saith the Lord: "No Cliques!"*

Group Interaction: A work session to put safeguards in place to eliminate favoritism.

1. Materials (Optional)

- Video clip from Walt Disney's movie *Cinderella*, Chapter 7-8, "Cat and Mouse," "Lady Tremaine"—DVD counter cues 00:20:41 to 00:23:28.
- Items that depict a few of your favorite things

2. Optional Openings

Video Clip: Show the opening scene from Walt Disney's *Cinderella*, which illustrates what it feels like to be the child who's overlooked.

Visual Illustration: Display your favorite things, and explain why each is your favorite.

3. Digging In

Personal Story: Share a story about inappropriate favoritism.

4. Digging Deeper

James 2:1-4

5. Taking It Inward

Imitating God's heart for the poor

6. Wrapping It Up

Challenge: Poverty shows up in more ways than lack of riches, giving favoritism a chance to show up more often than we think.

SESSION 5

Setting the Heart

In an intimate conversation with his closest friends, Jesus made an outlandish promise. Read his words from John 14:21 and note what the Lord said would happen if his disciples followed God through on a few key actions.

> "Whoever has my commands and obeys them, he is the one who loves me. He who loves me will be loved by my Father, and I too will love him and show myself to him." (John 14:21)

Let's get this straight. In the passage above, underline the two things we can do to show our love for Jesus. Then circle three things we'll enjoy when we have and obey Jesus' commands. Did you catch the third one—that Jesus will show himself to us? When was the last time Jesus really showed himself to you? Don't explain away that verse, thinking that Jesus is talking about his second coming—the day when he'll show himself to all the earth. He's talking about here and now, and it sounds like a fairly conspicuous manifestation!

While the book of James doesn't contain the spoken commands of Jesus, we can certainly apply Jesus' promise from John 14:21. Make today's session preparation a time dedicated to having (*owning*) Jesus' commands as revealed through the book of James. Let's commit to obeying whatever he impresses on our hearts, even if it's the subtlest impression. Then look for an outpouring of love from Jesus and the Father. And expect the outlandish—a personal revelation of Jesus to you! It's a great promise—but don't neglect your part of the bargain.

Digging In

It's a Straight Line from Faith to Deeds

You may have noted that throughout his letter, James resolved nearly every dilemma by calling for tangible, visible behavior from his readers—actions that could be seen—like doing what the Word says, looking after widows and orphans, and refraining from favoritism.

Read James 2:14-26 from your Scripture sheets. Use your colored pencils to uniquely mark the words *faith* and *deeds* (including synonyms like *works* and *action*).

After you've read and marked the passage, look back at the verses that mention both faith and deeds/works/action. List in the following space everything James says about the relationship between the two.

Insight

Faith Versus Works—or Faith and Works?

Faith versus works constitutes one of the great debates of the Christian age. After reading James 2, people often ask questions like: *Isn't salvation a free gift, dependent on our faith, not works? What about Romans 5:1: "Since we have been justified through faith, we have peace with God through our Lord Jesus Christ"?* Let's sort it out.

> **Paul says:**
> "Therefore, since we have been justified through faith, we have peace with God through our Lord Jesus Christ." (Romans 5:1)
>
> "For it is by grace you have been saved, through faith—and this not from yourselves, it is the gift of God—not by works, so that no one can boast." (Ephesians 2:8-9)
>
> **James says:**
> "You see that a person is justified by what he does and not by faith alone." (James 2:24)

At a glance, Paul and James seem to contradict one another. The great reformer Martin Luther thought, because of this apparent contradiction, the book of James should have been removed from the canon of Scripture. (He made such statements in the preface of an early edition of the Luther Bible but removed them in later editions.)

The irony is that both Paul and Luther were experiencing similar circumstances. In Paul's day, the people—Jews and deceived Gentiles—were using works of the law for salvation. In Luther's day it was the works of the church that the people relied on. In both cases, these works were not the same deeds spoken of by James.

Throughout the New Testament, when Paul refers to works, he means works of the law—works that the Jews and legalistic Gentiles performed *in order to achieve* salvation. When James speaks of works, he means deeds done *as a result of* salvation. You can categorize the two types of works this way: works done before salvation, which are useless in terms of securing salvation, and works done after salvation, which are useful in that they please God and fulfill the mission of Christ.

In your own words, what's the connection between faith and deeds?

Cross-Checking

Define the Deeds

The following passages give a more complete picture of the relationship between faith and deeds. Read these from your Bible, carefully observing the context of each passage. Then record in the columns anything you learn about the works or deeds mentioned. (The New International Version often uses the phrase *observing the law*.)

Bible Verses	Deeds We're to Do	Cautions about Our Deeds
Matthew 25:31-46		
John 3:21		
Romans 3:20-28		
Galatians 2:15-16		
Galatians 5:6		

Ephesians 2:8-10 (note verse 10)		
Titus 3:8		

Circle anything you recorded in the chart that parallels James' take on deeds in James 2.

Based on your study so far, what kinds of deeds are we asked to do?

In your own words, write the definitive conclusion James makes about the connection between faith and actions in James 2:22.

Taking It Inward

Your Faith: Taking Its Vital Signs

You might say that Paul and James address two extremes of a single perspective. Paul was speaking to new believers who felt compelled to observe the law to achieve or maintain a saving relationship with God. James was encouraging established believers to see that true faith led to action. After all, if faith doesn't result in action, can you really call it faith? People can say that they believe in exercise for physical fitness, but if they're unwilling to go to the fitness center or do any exercise, what good is their belief? How does anyone know they believe in fitness?

Every one of us is capable of living at either extreme. We can think our good works save us, or we can blow them off as unimportant in comparison with our faith in Christ. Take a minute or two to reflect on your own faith in Jesus.

> Since faith without action is dead, what's the medical condition of your faith? Base your answer solely on your actions.

> ☐ dead
> ☐ on life support
> ☐ in the intensive care unit
> ☐ in the emergency room
> ☐ alive and kickin'
> ☐ showing improvement in vital signs
> ☐ showing symptoms of sickness

> Here's a tough question—one you may be tempted to skip. But don't. If your faith in Jesus Christ is not leading to action, could it be that you *really don't believe*? Deal with this question honestly before continuing. Write your thoughts.

Wrapping It Up

Do Good, and Do It Secretly

In chapter 2 James uses three examples to illustrate the kinds of deeds he's talking about. Write them down in the first column. Think about the first item you've written down. What general type of deed is this or what is a key characteristic of it? Write that in the second column. Answer the same question for James' other examples. Then give examples of things we might do today that are similar to the biblical examples. Write those in the third column.

If you need to refresh your memory about Rahab, read Joshua 2.

James' Illustrations	Types or Characteristics	Corresponding Deeds for Today

James' illustrations give us a great jump start on backing our faith with action; we don't have to search for ideas. There's no excuse for not locking on to a practical task that can put action to your faith: Do something about the physical needs of a brother or sister in Christ before the session with your students. Do it in secret—and keep it a secret!

Before you close your book, select the appropriate Teach It guide for your session. (Full Teach It guides are on the CD-ROM accompanying this book.) Then read through the guide so you're familiar with the flow of the session and confident with each exercise. Be sure to allow time for printing or photocopying the Scripture sheets and student journal pages, and pulling together any materials needed.

Finish your time by praying for your students—that they will be open to honestly evaluating their faith and see that meaningful faith generates activity.

WEB SUPPORT:
Don't forget to check out Web support for *Hear and Do* at www.inword.org. You'll find updated media suggestions such as music and video clips along with more prep helps and specific application ideas. Look for the Digging Deeper series icon. You'll find password information in the Instructions at the front of this book.

1. Materials

For this session each student will need—
- the James 2 Scripture sheet
- the student journal page for Session 5
- his or her journal pages from Sessions 1-4
- his or her own Bible, pen, and notebook

You'll also need—
- a whiteboard and markers
- colored pencils (at least two colors per student)
- video option: a clip, from a video-sharing Web site such as YouTube, illustrating the connection between faith and deeds; use search words like *faith, deeds, with* or *without*. To search for one specific clip you might find helpful, add *Mountain View Wesleyan Church* to the other search words.
- audio option: the song "Deeds" by Sanctus Real

2. Session Intro

GOALS OF SESSION 5

As students experience this session, they will—
- explore the relationship between real faith and real action.
- apply specific actions, in today's terms, to deeds we're told to do in Scripture.
- evaluate the vital signs of their faith, knowing that faith without deeds is a flat-line faith.

PRAYER

OPEN: *TRACK THE THEMES*

Group Interaction: Recap the big themes in James with your students.
Video Option: Show a video clip connecting faith and deeds.
Music Option: Make the connection between faith and deeds by playing the song "Deeds" by Sanctus Real found on the *Fight the Tide* album.

3. Digging In: *It's a Straight Line from Faith to Deeds*

Group Dig: Explore James 2:14-26 to find the connection James makes between faith and deeds.

4. Cross-Checking: *Define the Deeds*

Personal Retreat: Does Scripture contradict itself on the relationship between faith and deeds? You decide.

5. Taking It Inward: *Do Good and Do It Secretly*

Group Interaction: As a group, process the kind of deeds James is talking about and compile a list of what these deeds look like today.

6. Wrapping It Up: *Needs and Deeds*

Group Interaction: Brainstorm ways to encourage each other to keep commitments to the actions James is leading you to do.

1. Materials

For this session each student will need—
- the James 2 Scripture sheet
- the student journal page for Session 5
- his or her journal pages from Sessions 1-4
- his or her own Bible, pen, and notebook

You'll also need—
- a whiteboard and markers
- colored pencils (at least two colors per student)
- video option: a clip, from a video-sharing Web site such as YouTube, illustrating the connection between faith and deeds; use search words like *faith, deeds, with,* or *without*. To search for one specific clip you might find helpful, add *Mountain View Wesleyan Church* to the other search words.
- music option: the song "Deeds" by Sanctus Real

2. Session Intro

GOALS OF SESSION 5
As students experience this session, they will—
- explore the relationship between real faith and real action.
- apply specific actions, in today's terms, to deeds we're told to do in Scripture.
- evaluate the vital signs of their faith, knowing that faith without deeds is a flat-line faith.

PRAYER

OPEN: *TRACK THE THEMES*
Group Interaction: Recap with your students the big themes in James.
Video Option: Show a video clip connecting faith and deeds.
Music Option: Make the connection between faith and deeds by playing the song "Deeds" by Sanctus Real found on the *Fight the Tide* album.

3. Digging In: *It's a Straight Line from Faith to Deeds*

Group Dig: Explore James 2:14-26 to find the connection James makes between faith and deeds.

4. Cross-Checking: *Define the Deeds*

Personal Retreat: Does Scripture contradict itself on the relationship between faith and deeds? You decide.

5. Taking It Inward: *Do Good and Do It Secretly*

Group Interaction: As a group, process the kind of deeds James is talking about and compile a list of what these deeds look like today.

Large-Group Option: Divide into small groups to process the kind of deeds James is talking about and compile a list of what these deeds look like today.

6. Wrapping It Up: *Needs and Deeds*

Group Interaction: Brainstorm ways to encourage each other to keep commitments to the actions James is leading you to do.

JAMES 2:14-26
FAITH YOU CAN SEE

1. Materials

For this session each student will need—
- the James 2 Scripture sheet
- the student journal page for Session 5
- his or her journal pages from Sessions 1-4
- his or her own Bible, pen, and notebook

You'll also need—
- a whiteboard and markers
- colored pencils (at least two colors per student)

2. Session Intro

GOALS OF SESSION 5

As students experience this session, they will—
- explore the relationship between real faith and real action.
- apply specific actions, in today's terms, to deeds we're told to do in Scripture.
- evaluate the vital signs of their faith, knowing that faith without deeds is a flat-line faith.

PRAYER

OPEN: *TRACK THE THEMES*
Group Interaction: Recap with your students the big themes in James.

3. Digging In: *It's a Straight Line from Faith to Deeds*

Group Dig: Explore James 2:14-26 to find the connection James makes between faith and deeds.

4. Cross-Checking: *Define the Deeds*

Personal Retreat: Does Scripture contradict itself on the relationship between faith and deeds? You decide.

5. Taking It Inward: *Do Good and Do It Secretly*

Group Interaction: As a group, process the kind of deeds James is talking about and compile a list of what these deeds look like today.

6. Wrapping It Up: *Needs and Deeds*

Group Interaction: Brainstorm ways to encourage each other to keep commitments to the actions James is leading you to do.

1. Materials

For this session each student will need—
- the James 2 Scripture sheet
- the student journal page for Session 5
- his or her journal pages from Sessions 1-4
- his or her own Bible, pen, and notebook

You'll also need—
- a whiteboard and markers
- colored pencils (at least two colors per student)

2. Session Intro

GOALS OF SESSION 5

As students experience this session, they will—
- explore the relationship between real faith and real action.
- apply specific actions, in today's terms, to deeds we're told to do in Scripture.
- evaluate the vital signs of their faith, knowing that faith without deeds is a flat-line faith.

PRAYER

OPEN: *TRACK THE THEMES*
Group Interaction: Recap with your students the big themes in James.

3. Digging In: *It's a Straight Line from Faith to Deeds*

Group Dig: Explore James 2:14-26 to find the connection James makes between faith and deeds.

4. Cross-Checking: *Define the Deeds*

Personal Retreat: Does Scripture contradict itself on the relationship between faith and deeds? You decide.

5. Taking It Inward: *Do Good and Do It Secretly*

Group Interaction: As a group, process the kind of deeds James is talking about and compile a list of what these deeds look like today.

6. Wrapping It Up: *Needs and Deeds*

Group Interaction: Brainstorm ways to encourage each other to keep commitments to the actions James is leading you to do.

JAMES 2:14-26
FAITH YOU CAN SEE

1. Materials

For this session each student will need—
- his or her own Bible and pen
- the student journal page for Session 5 (Using the student journal page is *not* optional for this session.)

You'll also need—
- a pack of pencils with erasers
- optional: a few spare Bibles for students who've forgotten theirs

2. Session Intro

GOALS OF SESSION 5
As students experience this session, they will—
- explore the relationship between real faith and real action.
- apply specific actions, in today's terms, to deeds we're told to do in Scripture.
- evaluate the vital signs of their faith, knowing that faith without deeds is a flat-line faith.

PRAYER

OPEN: *TRACK THE THEMES*
Group Interaction: Recap with your students the big themes in James.

3. Digging In: *It's a Straight Line from Faith to Deeds*

Group Dig: Explore James 2:14-26 to find the connection James makes between faith and deeds.

4. Cross-Checking: *Define the Deeds*

Personal Retreat: Does Scripture contradict itself on the relationship between faith and deeds? You decide.

5. Taking It Inward: *Do Good and Do It Secretly*

Group Interaction: As a group, process the kind of deeds James is talking about and compile a list of what these deeds look like today.

6. Wrapping It Up: *Needs and Deeds*

Group Interaction: Brainstorm ways to encourage each other to keep commitments to the actions James is leading you to do.

1. Materials (Optional)

- Three or four students to catch you in the game *Trust Fall*
- An order of french fries from a fast-food restaurant

2. Optional Openings

Visual Illustration: Share announcements or start your talk while in *Trust Fall* position.
Quotations: Share the quotations to introduce the idea of supporting your ideals and convictions with action.

3. Digging In

Personal Story: Share a personal story that involves the relationship between bragging (trash-talk) and the ability (or inability) to back up the talk.

4. Digging Deeper

James 2:14-17: Continue your personal story, talking about the importance of putting action to your beliefs.

5. Taking It Inward

Visual Illustration: How is a bag of french fries like trusting God?

6. Wrapping It Up

If you say you love someone but do nothing for him or her, do you really love that person, or are your words empty? If we say we believe but do nothing for Jesus, do we really believe?

Setting the Heart

Proverbs 2:1-5, a passage we read in Session 1, tells us we'll find the knowledge of God if we store up his commands inside us. Jesus, in dismissing an accusation from the Pharisees, gives another clue as to how our behavior will change when we store up the right stuff within us.

> You brood of vipers, how can you who are evil say anything good? For out of the overflow of the heart the mouth speaks. The good man brings good things out of the good stored up in him, and the evil man brings evil things out of the evil stored up in him. But I tell you that men will have to give account on the day of judgment for every careless word they have spoken. For by your words you will be acquitted, and by your words you will be condemned. (Matthew 12:34-37)

As the Spirit softens your heart in today's study of God's Word, don't overlook one of the most fundamental applications for anything we learn from Scripture—the words we speak. As you'll see in James 3, if God's people could just master this problem area, the world would be a much better place.

Digging In

What James Wrote about Tongues

Read James 3:1-12 using your Scripture sheets. As you read, draw a tongue  or lips over every mention of the tongue.

Then look back at your markings, and make a detailed list of everything James teaches concerning the tongue.

James uses three illustrations in verses 3-5 to make his point about the tongue. Each illustration consists of a small item that controls a larger item. Record these in the following space.

Small Items   **Large Items**

Reread James 3:1-12. This time look for anything specific James' readers may have been doing to warrant such stern warnings about their tongues.

Taking It Inward

Big Damage Done by Fire, Hurricanes—and Tongues

Think for a minute about any recent situations in which you saw someone's tongue spark forest-fire-sized damage. (Write in code if someone else will be reading this.)

Have you ever been guilty of using your tongue in the same manner as James' readers—to curse people, who are made in God's image?

It's worth noting that James doesn't appear to be referring only to fellow believers. The word *men* in verse 9 implies people outside the church as well as brothers and sisters in Christ. Consider this scenario: Have you ever observed the downfall of notorious unbelievers (such as philanderers, pornographers, unethical employers, deceptive politicians, and the like) and expressed that they're getting what they deserved? Yet, as difficult as it might be to embrace, they too are made in God's likeness. Do we somehow rationalize that it's okay to curse these kinds of people? Note your thoughts.

You should have listed about seven observations in the first exercise (Digging In) of this session, looking at what James teaches us about the tongue. Circle two items: the one you find the most insightful and the one that most convicts you. We'll come back to these in a few minutes.

Cross-Checking

A Tongue Questionnaire

As you read the following Bible verses, look for the answers to the questions in the chart. (Each passage will not necessarily answer every question.)

	How can the tongue be used destructively?	How can the tongue be used constructively?	What is the source of what the mouth speaks?
Proverbs 16:28			
Proverbs 17:9			
Matthew 12:33-37			
Romans 10:8-10			
Ephesians 4:29			
Ephesians 6:19-20			

Taking It Inward

The Power of Your Tongue

How does your tongue spend most of its time?
- ☐ praising God
- ☐ cursing man
- ☐ declaring the mysteries of the gospel

If even 1 percent of your time is spent cursing man, James 3:9-12 speaks directly to your situation. Write down the examples James gave of things that don't mix.

In what areas of your speech do you struggle most?
- ☐ lying
- ☐ telling half-truths
- ☐ presenting people, sometimes even friends, in a negative light
- ☐ talking about others' struggles and mistakes
- ☐ putting myself in a positive light at the expense of someone else
- ☐ passing along information about people to others
- ☐ other (name it)

Earlier you were asked to circle two observations in your list about the tongue—one that you found most insightful, one that was most convicting. Take a moment to pray about these two truths, asking the Lord to give you wisdom about how to reflect the behavior he desires. (Remember what God promised concerning wisdom in James 1:5.)

What's your tongue going to be? The following two options, which James mentioned, cannot coexist. You might think you can do both, but when you try to praise God with the same mouth you've used to curse people, God won't hear it as praise. He'll only hear empty words. So, which is it going to be? Pick one.

- Do you want to be an uplifting vessel who praises God, encourages others, and declares the message of the gospel? or
- Do you want to be an unwholesome vessel who curses men and divides friends?

Wrapping It Up

Say and Do Faith

Commit yourself to doing the right thing. Consider what could happen in the church and in the world if God's people—starting with you and your student ministry—would obey these truths about the tongue.

Select the appropriate Teach It guide for your session. (Full Teach It guides are on the CD-ROM accompanying this book.) Then read through the guide so you're familiar with the flow of the session and confident with each exercise. Be sure to allow time for printing or photocopying the Scripture sheets and student journal pages, and pulling together any materials needed.

Finish your time by praying that your students would see the connection between the heart and the tongue and be motivated to use the tongue for positive impact.

WEB SUPPORT:
Don't forget to check out Web support for *Hear and Do* at www.inword.org. You'll find updated media suggestions such as music and video clips along with more prep helps and specific application ideas. Look for the Digging Deeper series icon. You'll find password information in the Instructions at the front of this book.

1. Materials

For this session each student will need—
- the James 3 Scripture sheet
- the student journal page for Session 6
- his or her own Bible, pen, and notebook

You'll also need—
- a whiteboard and markers
- colored pencils (at least one color per student)
- video clip of a giraffe tongue from a video-sharing Web site like YouTube
- images depicting the various illustrations of the tongue found in James (see Digging In). Do an Internet search for these ahead of time and print or project them
- images of a Clydesdale horse, a bit, a rudder, a ship, a spark, and a forest fire. A model of a ship with a rudder, an actual horse's bit, and a book of matches could be used as tangible props.

2. Session Intro

GOALS OF SESSION 6
As students experience this session, they will—
- discover the power of the tongue.
- explore the constructive and destructive uses of the tongue.
- be challenged to initiate a practical plan based on James' instructions regarding the tongue.

PRAYER

OPEN: *TONGUE TRIVIA*
Group Interaction: Have a *longest tongue* contest.
Video Option: Show some surprising video of a giraffe's tongue.
Trivia: Share some interesting trivia about tongues.

3. Digging In: *What James Wrote about Tongues*

Group Dig: Explore James 3:1-12 to see what James has to say about the tongue.

4. Taking It Inward: *Big Damage Done by Fire, Hurricanes—and Tongues*

Group Interaction: Share with each other about being the victim—or the perpetrator—of a calamity started by a tongue.

5. Cross-Checking: *A Tongue Questionnaire*

Personal Retreat: Explore other verses that teach us how the tongue can be used for constructive or destructive purposes.

6. Taking It Inward: *The Power of Your Tongue*

Group Interaction: Help each other create an action plan for obeying God's instructions concerning our tongues.

7. Wrapping It Up: *Say and Do Faith*

Group Interaction: Challenge students with the fact that we display our faith in only two ways: what we do and what we say.

JAMES 3:1-12
FAITH YOU CAN SAY

1. Materials

For this session each student will need—
- the James 3 Scripture sheet
- the student journal page for Session 6
- his or her own Bible, pen, and notebook

You'll also need—
- a whiteboard and markers
- colored pencils (at least one color per student)
- info for *Tongue Trivia*
- Large-Group Option: butcher paper for a wall-sized Scripture sheet and a large-tip marker

2. Session Intro

GOALS OF SESSION 6

As students experience this session, they will—
- discover the power of the tongue.
- explore the constructive and destructive uses of the tongue.
- be challenged to initiate a practical plan based on James' instructions regarding the tongue.

PRAYER

OPEN: *TONGUE TRIVIA*

Group Interaction: Have a *longest tongue* contest.
Video Option: Show some surprising video of a giraffe's tongue.
Trivia: Share some interesting trivia about tongues.

3. Digging In: *What James Wrote about Tongues*

Group Dig: Explore James 3:1-12 to see what James has to say about the tongue.
Large-Group Option: Create a wall-size Scripture sheet for the group to read and mark together.

4. Taking It Inward: *Big Damage Done by Fire, Hurricanes—and Tongues*

Group Interaction: Share with each other about being the victim—or the perpetrator—of a calamity started by a tongue.

5. Cross-Checking: *A Tongue Questionnaire*

Personal Retreat: Explore other verses that teach us how the tongue can be used for constructive or destructive purposes.

Large-Group Option: Students will process Cross-Checking questions in small groups before gathering as a large group for Taking It Inward.

6. Taking It Inward: *The Power of Your Tongue*

Group Interaction: Help each other create an action plan for obeying God's instructions concerning our tongues.

7. Wrapping It Up: *Say and Do Faith*

Group Interaction: Challenge students with the fact that we display our faith in only two ways: what we do and what we say.

1. Materials

For this session each student will need—
- the James 3 Scripture sheet
- the student journal page for Session 6
- his or her own Bible, pen, and notebook

You'll also need—
- a whiteboard and markers
- colored pencils (at least one color per student)
- info for *Tongue Trivia*

2. Session Intro

GOALS OF SESSION 6
As students experience this session, they will—
- discover the power of the tongue.
- explore the constructive and destructive uses of the tongue.
- be challenged to initiate a practical plan based on James' instructions regarding the tongue.

PRAYER

OPEN: *TONGUE TRIVIA*
Trivia: Share some interesting trivia about tongues.

3. Digging In: *What James Wrote about Tongues*

Group Dig: Explore James 3:1-12 to see what James has to say about the tongue.

4. Taking It Inward: *Big Damage Done by Fire, Hurricanes—and Tongues*

Group Interaction: Share with each other about being the victim—or the perpetrator—of a calamity started by a tongue.

5. Cross-Checking: *A Tongue Questionnaire*

Personal Retreat: Explore other verses that teach us how the tongue can be used for constructive or destructive purposes.

6. Taking It Inward: *The Power of Your Tongue*

Group Interaction: Help each other create an action plan for obeying God's instructions concerning our tongues.

7. Wrapping It Up: *Say and Do Faith*

Group Interaction: Challenge students with the fact that we display our faith in only two ways: what we do and what we say.

1. Materials

For this session each student will need—
- the James 3 Scripture sheet
- the student journal page for Session 6
- his or her own Bible, pen, and notebook

You'll also need—
- a whiteboard and markers
- colored pencils (at least one color per student)
- info for *Tongue Trivia*

2. Session Intro

GOALS OF SESSION 6
As students experience this session, they will—
- discover the power of the tongue.
- explore the constructive and destructive uses of the tongue.
- be challenged to initiate a practical plan based on James' instructions regarding the tongue.

PRAYER

OPEN: *TONGUE TRIVIA*
Trivia: Share some interesting trivia about tongues.

3. Digging In: *What James Wrote about Tongues*

Group Dig: Explore James 3:1-12 to see what James has to say about the tongue.

4. Taking It Inward: *Big Damage Done by Fire, Hurricanes—and Tongues*

Group Interaction: Share with each other about being the victim—or the perpetrator—of a calamity started by a tongue.

5. Cross-Checking: *A Tongue Questionnaire*

Personal Retreat: Explore other verses that teach us how the tongue can be used for constructive or destructive purposes.

6. Taking It Inward: *The Power of Your Tongue*

Group Interaction: Help each other create an action plan for obeying God's instructions concerning our tongues.

7. Wrapping It Up: *Say and Do Faith*

Group Interaction: Challenge students with the fact that we display our faith in only two ways: what we do and what we say.

1. Materials

For this session each student will need—
- his or her own Bible and pen
- optional: journal page for Session 6 (Using the student journal page is optional in the coffeehouse setting because table space may be limited.)

You'll also need—
- a pack of pencils with erasers
- optional: a few spare Bibles for students who've forgotten theirs
- info for *Tongue Trivia*

2. Session Intro

GOALS OF SESSION 6

As students experience this session, they will—
- discover the power of the tongue.
- explore the constructive and destructive uses of the tongue.
- be challenged to initiate a practical plan based on James' instructions regarding the tongue.

PRAYER

OPEN: *TONGUE TRIVIA*
Trivia: Share some interesting trivia about tongues.

3. Digging In: *What James Wrote about Tongues*

Group Dig: Explore James 3:1-12 to see what James has to say about the tongue.

4. Taking It Inward: *Big Damage Done by Fire, Hurricanes—and Tongues*

Group Interaction: Share with each other about being the victim—or the perpetrator—of a calamity started by a tongue.

5. Taking It Inward: *A Tongue Questionnaire*

Group Interaction: Evaluate with each other how your recent tongue usage compares with James' instructions regarding the tongue.

6. Cross-Checking: *The Power of Your Tongue*

Group Interaction: Using Ephesians 4:29, help each other create an action plan for obeying God's instructions concerning our tongues.

7. Wrapping It Up: *Say and Do Faith*

Group Interaction: Challenge students with the fact that we display our faith in only two ways: what we do and what we say.

1. Materials (Optional)

- Two or three complicated phrases for a few rounds of the game *Telephone*
- A table set with six tubes of toothpaste and six plastic bowls for a game called *Toothpaste Squeeze*

2. Optional Openings

Quotations: Share a few quotations about talk and the tongue.
Group Interaction: The game *Telephone*
Group Interaction: Play the *Toothpaste Squeeze* game to illustrate how easy it is to get toothpaste out of the tube, but how difficult it is to get it back in.

3. Digging In

Personal Story: Share a story about when you were hurt by words spoken to you.

4. Digging Deeper

James 3:9-12

5. Wrapping It Up

Challenge students that they must choose how they're going to use their tongues: either for constructive or destructive purposes. You can't have it both ways.

Setting the Heart

Paul warns that knowledge alone won't do us much good.

> We know that we all possess knowledge. Knowledge puffs up, but love builds up. (1 Corinthians 8:1)

As you study the Bible and encourage students to follow your lead, don't ever forget—or underestimate—the transformational power of God's Word. Scripture does more than enlarge our knowledge base. It actually rewires our inside—which soon shows up on the outside. Read the following verses from Psalm 19 and catch how God's Word (referred to as his law, precepts, ordinances, and so forth) is described. Also see what it has the power to do.

> The law of the LORD is perfect, reviving the soul. The statutes of the LORD are trustworthy, making wise the simple. The precepts of the LORD are right, giving joy to the heart. The commands of the LORD are radiant, giving light to the eyes. The fear of the LORD is pure, enduring forever. The ordinances of the LORD are sure and altogether righteous. They are more precious than gold, than much pure gold; they are sweeter than honey, than honey from the comb. By them is your servant warned; in keeping them there is great reward. (Psalm 19:7-11)

One benefit the psalmist mentions goes right along with James 3—God's statutes are trustworthy, making wise the simple. We all want more wisdom. But what we forget is that wisdom can come from two directions—above and below. Earthly wisdom looks tempting because it appeals to the flesh and typically involves a shortcut. And that's precisely the trap James wants us to avoid.

Digging In

Two Kinds of Wisdom

Read James 3:13-18 using your Scripture sheets. As you read, look for two types of wisdom—good wisdom and bad wisdom. Mark each in a unique way.

After you've read and marked the passage, list everything you learn about each kind of wisdom.

Good wisdom   **Bad wisdom**

In verse 17, James lists several behavior traits that accompany wisdom from heaven. List these in the first column of the following chart. For now, ignore the remaining columns.

Behavior Traits of Wisdom	Situation _____	Situation _____	Situation _____

Cross-Checking

Why God Is Bullish on Wisdom

Since wisdom is one of the awesome characteristics of God, you might guess that this subject is dealt with in countless Scripture passages. We'll spare you the trouble of looking up all of them (you can thank us later) and instead focus on just one. Read 1 Kings 3:4-14 from your Bible. As you read, look for answers to these questions:

What did Solomon ask for?

Why did God like this request?

How did God respond?

You'll recall that James mentioned wisdom earlier in his letter. Read James 1:5-8 again and answer these questions:

What did James say to ask for?

How will God respond?

What similarities or parallels do you see between James' teaching on wisdom and Solomon's request?

Based on your study thus far, why do you think God is so pro-wisdom?

When it's God's wisdom we're talking about—wisdom from above—what kind of behavior accompanies it?

Why would God want this behavior to be associated with his wisdom?

Digging Deeper

Test-Drive Wisdom (Go Ahead—Take It for a Spin)

When you're experiencing a conflict with another person, whose interests do you usually have in mind? If you're completely honest, you'll probably admit that you often put your own interests ahead of the interests of others. Look closely at James 3:14-16.

What does this type of wisdom degenerate into?

List here any situations (job, ministry, relationships, decisions to make) where you could use a dose of wisdom from heaven.

Now look back at the traits that accompany heavenly wisdom. You listed them in the chart at the beginning of this lesson. Here's an example of how you can evaluate your situation based on those traits: Let's say you're the youth director of a church, and you'd like to do a major outreach event. You've already done some legwork to bring in a band and a speaker and to offer loads of food. Since your church has never done something of this magnitude, not everyone is supportive of your idea. In fact, you're encountering some resistance. You're not sure how to proceed—but luckily you've studied James 3. What questions can you ask to evaluate the situation based on each trait? The following chart gives some possibilities.

Wisdom Trait	Your Situation
pure	What are your motives? Are they pure? Are you planning this event out of a broken heart for the lost and obedience to a prompting from God? Are you privately pleased about the increase of your personal visibility or praise for your ministry or program?
peace-loving	When you imagine meeting with key board members or staff on this subject, do you picture a confrontation? Have you thought about how you can share your vision without being combative?
considerate	In his book *The Seven Habits of Highly Effective People*, Stephen R. Covey says, "Seek first to understand, then to be understood." A great maxim! Are you being quick to listen and slow to speak (James 1:19)?
submissive	Do you have the support of your pastoral leadership? Are you operating in submission to those who have authority over you?
full of mercy	If the event happens and is a huge success, will you in any way communicate a *See? I told you so!* attitude? Will you view success as an opportunity to advance your agenda?
full of good fruit	As you interact with those who are resistant to your ideas, will they leave your presence affirmed and encouraged in their walk with Jesus? Or will they head home to reload for the next confrontation?

impartial	Are you open to the possibility you may be wrong?
sincere	Do you view people who are resistant as having legitimate concerns, or do you see them as commodities to be persuaded (or manipulated) to your way of thinking?

Now it's your turn to give it a spin. In the chart at the beginning of this lesson, write three of your current situations in the column headings. Then apply the traits of godly wisdom to each situation, just as we did in the sample. Let the Holy Spirit teach you through this exercise; there may be a thing or two he's been itching to say.

Finally, note the promise in James 3:18—in fact, write it here.

WEB SUPPORT:
Don't forget to check out Web support for *Hear and Do* at www.inword. org. You'll find updated media suggestions such as music and video clips along with more prep helps and specific application ideas. Look for the Digging Deeper series icon. You'll find password information in the Instructions at the front of this book.

Wrapping It Up

Just Ask!

Has this study brought to mind any recent occasions when you acted out of earthly wisdom? If so, remember that God loves a repentant heart. Before you get with your group, get right with God and others. Ask the forgiveness of anyone you've dealt with out of earthly wisdom.

Before you close your book, select the appropriate Teach It guide for your session. (Full Teach It guides are on the CD-ROM accompanying this book.) Then read through the guide so you're familiar with the flow of the session and confident with each exercise. Be sure to allow time for printing or photocopying the Scripture sheets and student journal pages, and pulling together any materials needed.

Finish your prep time by praying for the students in your group. Pray that they will see the areas in their lives that need godly wisdom and that they'll be motivated to ask God for a generous portion.

1. Materials

For this session each student will need—
- the James 3 Scripture sheet
- the student journal page for Session 7
- his or her own Bible, pen, and notebook

You'll also need—
- a whiteboard and markers
- colored pencils (at least two colors per student)
- a deck or two of playing cards, alphabet flash cards, or other similar cards

2. Session Intro

GOALS OF SESSION 7

As students experience this session, they will—
- discover why wisdom is one of God's favorite things to give.
- explore the many ways God's wisdom can be put to use.
- take time during the session to pray specifically for wisdom.

PRAYER

OPEN: *WISDOM MEMORY GAME*
Group Interaction: Lead the group in a few rounds of a version of *The Memory Game*.

3. Digging In: *Two Kinds of Wisdom*

Group Dig: Explore James 3:13-18 to see what James has to say about two kinds of wisdom that are easily accessible to us.

4. Cross-Checking: *Why God Is Bullish on Wisdom*

Group Drama: Use some improvisation to see the similarities between the wisdom of James and Solomon.

5. Taking It Inward: *Test-Drive Wisdom (Go Ahead—Take It for a Spin)*

Personal Retreat: Give wisdom a try in areas that could use a good dose of wisdom from above.

6. Wrapping It Up: *Just Ask!*

Group Prayer: God says he gives wisdom generously when we ask. Go ahead and take him up on that offer.

1. Materials

For this session each student will need—
- the James 3 Scripture sheet
- the student journal page for Session 7
- his or her own Bible, pen, and notebook

You'll also need—
- a whiteboard and markers
- colored pencils (at least two colors per student)
- video clip: a clip of stupid human tricks from a video-sharing Web site such as YouTube

2. Session Intro

GOALS OF SESSION 7

As students experience this session, they will—
- discover why wisdom is one of God's favorite things to give.
- explore the many ways God's wisdom can be put to use.
- take time during the session to pray specifically for wisdom.

PRAYER

OPEN: *WISDOM BRAINSTORM*

Group Interaction: Show a video clip of stupid human tricks and then brainstorm about wisdom, discussing the difference between wisdom and intelligence.

3. Digging In: *Two Kinds of Wisdom*

Group Dig: Explore James 3:13-18 to see what James has to say about two kinds of wisdom that are easily accessible to us.

4. Cross-Checking: *Why God Is Bullish on Wisdom*

Group Dig: Investigate the similarities between the wisdom of James and of Solomon.

5. Taking It Inward: *Test-Drive Wisdom (Go Ahead—Take It for a Spin)*

Personal Retreat: Give wisdom a try in areas that could use a good dose of wisdom from above.

6. Wrapping It Up: *Just Ask!*

Group Prayer: God says he gives wisdom generously when we ask. Go ahead and take him up on that offer.

1. Materials

For this session each student will need—
- the James 3 Scripture sheet
- the student journal page for Session 7
- his or her own Bible, pen, and notebook

You'll also need—
- a whiteboard and markers
- colored pencils (at least two colors per student)
- optional: a clip of stupid human tricks from a video-sharing Web site such as YouTube

2. Session Intro

GOALS OF SESSION 7
As students experience this session, they will—
- discover why wisdom is one of God's favorite things to give.
- explore the many ways God's wisdom can be put to use.
- take time during the session to pray specifically for wisdom.

PRAYER

OPEN: *WISDOM BRAINSTORM*
Video Option: Show a video clip of stupid human tricks.
Group Interaction: Brainstorm about wisdom and discuss the difference between wisdom and intelligence.

3. Digging In: *Two Kinds of Wisdom*

Group Dig: Explore James 3:13-18 to see what James has to say about two kinds of wisdom that are easily accessible to us.

4. Cross-Checking: *Why God Is Bullish on Wisdom*

Group Read: Check out the similarities between the wisdom of James and of Solomon.

5. Taking It Inward: *Test-Drive Wisdom (Go Ahead—Take It for a Spin)*

Personal Retreat: Give wisdom a try in areas that could use a good dose of wisdom from above.

6. Wrapping It Up: *Just Ask!*

Group Prayer: God says he gives wisdom generously when we ask. Go ahead and take him up on that offer.

1. Materials

For this session each student will need—
- the James 3 Scripture sheet
- the student journal page for Session 7
- his or her own Bible, pen, and notebook

You'll also need—
- a whiteboard and markers
- colored pencils (at least two colors per student)

2. Session Intro

GOALS OF SESSION 7

As students experience this session, they will—
- discover why wisdom is one of God's favorite things to give.
- explore the many ways God's wisdom can be put to use.
- take time during the session to pray specifically for wisdom.

PRAYER

OPEN: *WISDOM BRAINSTORM*
Group Interaction: Brainstorm about wisdom and discuss the difference between wisdom and intelligence.

3. Digging In: *Two Kinds of Wisdom*

Group Dig: Explore James 3:13-18 to see what James has to say about two kinds of wisdom that are easily accessible to us.

4. Cross-Checking: *Why God Is Bullish on Wisdom*

Group Read: Check out the similarities between the wisdom of James and of Solomon.

5. Taking It Inward: *Test-Drive Wisdom (Go Ahead—Take It for a Spin)*

Personal Retreat: Give wisdom a try in areas that could use a good dose of wisdom from above.

6. Wrapping It Up: *Just Ask!*

Group Prayer: God says he gives wisdom generously when we ask. Go ahead and take him up on that offer.

1. Materials

For this session each student will need—
- his or her own Bible and pen
- optional: journal page for Session 7 (Using the student journal page is optional in the coffeehouse setting because table space may be limited.)

You'll also need—
- a pack of pencils with erasers
- optional: a few spare Bibles for students who've forgotten theirs

2. Session Intro

GOALS OF SESSION 7

As students experience this session, they will—
- discover why wisdom is one of God's favorite things to give.
- explore the many ways God's wisdom can be put to use.
- take time during the session to pray specifically for wisdom.

PRAYER

OPEN: *WISDOM BRAINSTORM*

Group Interaction: Brainstorm about wisdom and discuss the difference between wisdom and intelligence.

3. Digging In: *Two Kinds of Wisdom*

Group Dig: Explore James 3:13-18 to see what James has to say about two kinds of wisdom that are easily accessible to us.

4. Cross-Checking: *Why God Is Bullish on Wisdom*

Group Read: Check out the similarities between the wisdom of James and of Solomon.

5. Taking It Inward: *Test-Drive Wisdom (Go Ahead—Take It for a Spin)*

Group Interaction: Give wisdom a try in areas that could use a good dose of wisdom from above.

6. Wrapping It Up: *Just Ask!*

Group Prayer: God says he gives wisdom generously when we ask. Go ahead and take him up on that offer.

1. Materials (Optional)

- A small electric fan
- A small flag (or streamers or crepe paper)

2. Optional Openings

Visual Illustration: Use a fan and a flag to illustrate the properties of wind.
Quotations: Share a few quotations to get the group thinking about wisdom.

3. Digging In

Personal Story: Share a story about explaining wind to a child or about a time when you were fighting wind.
James 3:13-18

4. Digging Deeper

An endless supply of wisdom is closer than you think.

5. Wrapping It Up

Challenge students to begin applying God's wisdom to all their decisions.

SESSION 8

Setting the Heart

Authentic spiritual strength—with all its by-products—comes from lingering, intimate times with the Lord. A schedule packed with activity (even ministry) will deprive us of experiencing Jesus' living water where it flows the strongest and purest. We may actually become addicted to our busyness and, before long, the things of the world may become more and more enticing.

The author of Hebrews understood this truth. As you read the following verses, note how rest from busyness gives an opportunity to get maximum impact from the Word of God.

> There remains, then, a Sabbath-rest for the people of God; for anyone who enters God's rest also rests from his own work, just as God did from his. Let us, therefore, make every effort to enter that rest, so that no one will fall by following their example of disobedience. For the word of God is living and active. Sharper than any double-edged sword, it penetrates even to dividing soul and spirit, joints and marrow; it judges the thoughts and attitudes of the heart. (Hebrews 4:9-12)

Take a deep breath and release your grip on this day and its activities. You're about to hear James expound on a point similar to the one made in Hebrews. But don't think of this study time as preparation for ministry activity (leading your students). Think of it as a lingering, intimate time with the Savior. Enter his rest and give his Word maximum opportunity to penetrate your heart.

Digging In

We've Got a Few Problems Here

Read James 4:1-12 using your Scripture sheets. Circle every reference to the readers of the letter.

Once you've read and marked the passage, look back at what you circled. Note in the left-hand column of the following chart the problems James' readers were experiencing.

Problems	Instructions/Promises

In James 4:7-10 you saw a series of instructions and promises. Read the passage again, underlining the instructions in one color and the promises in another.

If the instructions and promises are offered as solutions to the problems (which is likely), what connection do you see between the problems mentioned in James 4:1-4 and the instructions and promises in verses 7-10? Take a minute to list the instructions and promises in the right-hand column above, writing them beside the problem they match best.

Cross-Checking

Then You Walked into the Sanctuary

Do you sense that James is asking his readers to refocus their eyes on things that are truly important? When we lose our intensity in following Jesus, our default settings tend to take over: selfish desires, earthly ambitions, longing for the things of the world rather than the things of God.

The author of Psalm 73, a Hebrew priest, had a similar problem. Read Psalm 73 twice from your Bible (it's short—just 28 verses). In your first read through, note the turning point that Asaph, the writer, experiences.

As you read the psalm a second time, list everything that describes Asaph and his perception of the world before the turning point and after it.

Before   **After**

What happened to Asaph between the before and the after? Write it word for word.

What similarities do you see between Asaph before his turning point and James' readers in James 4:1-4?

In what ways do the instructions and promises of James 4:7-10 show up in Psalm 73? Be specific.

How is your story similar to Asaph's? Are you involved in ministry as Asaph was, but not getting any true sanctuary time with God? Do you have moments when the things of the world look fulfilling—when you can't even remember why you're supposed to resist them?

Taking It Inward

Your Marching Orders: Submit, Resist, Come Near—and Lose That Pride

Perhaps James' instructions in verses 7-10 can serve as a basis for establishing real sanctuary time with God: submit to God, resist the Devil, come near to God, purify your heart, humble yourself. If we do these things, the Word promises that the Devil will flee, and God will come near and lift us up. That's a good deal! But our part of the equation is to obey the instructions.

List two or three things you can do to incorporate these instructions into your daily routine:

Submit to God and resist the Devil.

Come near to God.

Humble yourself before the Lord.

What are some areas of your life where genuine sanctuary time with God would be helpful? How would you like to experience the promises outlined in James 4? The following list contains several areas for personal meditation and prayer. Think about how you might apply the instructions from James to each area as you write your impressions.

My besetting sins and temptations

My prayer life

Decision making

Personal Bible study

Building relationships

Other

Wrapping It Up

Finding Your Own Sanctuary

Close your prep with some personal sanctuary time. The following passages support each instruction from James. Take some time to go through these passages and then expect to experience the promises from James—the Devil will flee, and God will come near and lift you up.

SUBMIT TO GOD/RESIST THE DEVIL
Romans 6:13; 1 Peter 5:6-10

COME NEAR TO GOD
Deuteronomy 4:29-31; Jeremiah 29:13; Hebrews 11:6

HUMBLE YOURSELF
Luke 14:7-14; Luke 18:9-14

Before you close your book, select the appropriate Teach It guide for your session. (Full Teach It guides are on the CD-ROM accompanying this book.) Then read through the guide so you're familiar with the flow of the session and confident with each exercise. Be sure to allow time for printing or photocopying the Scripture sheets and student journal pages, and pulling together any materials needed.

Finish your prep time by praying for your students, that they will be open to the truth God wants to pour into their hearts about spending sanctuary time with him.

WEB SUPPORT:
Don't forget to check out Web support for *Hear and Do* at www.inword.org. You'll find updated media suggestions such as music and video clips along with more prep helps and specific application ideas. Look for the Digging Deeper series icon. You'll find password information in the Instructions at the front of this book.

1. Materials

For this session each student will need—
- the James 4 Scripture sheet
- the student journal page for Session 8
- his or her own Bible, pen, and notebook

You'll also need—
- a whiteboard and markers
- colored pencils (at least two colors per student)
- worship tools: a media experience with songs and Scripture (see Wrapping It Up)

2. Session Intro

GOALS OF SESSION 8

As students experience this session, they will—
- explore the connection between sanctuary time with God and strength to beat temptation.
- discover the benefits of obeying God's instructions.
- practice creating a sanctuary experience with the group.

PRAYER

OPEN: *BUT IT'S A "GOOD BUSY"*

Group Interaction: Give students a chance to chart out a typical day to see how busy (or not busy) they are.

3. Digging In: *We've Got a Few Problems Here*

Group Dig: Explore James 4:1-12 to see what kind of problems James' readers were experiencing.

4. Cross-Checking: *Then You Walked into the Sanctuary*

Group Dig: Students will see that even Hebrew priests were tempted if they didn't get their time with God.

5. Taking It Inward: *Let's Hear It for Asaph!*

Group Interaction: What can Old Testament Asaph and New Testament James teach a 21st century student about following God?

6. Wrapping It Up: *Finding Your Own Sanctuary*

Sanctuary Options: Choose an option that will help your students begin experiencing the strength and power of true sanctuary time with God.

JAMES 4:1-12
SANCTUARY

1. Materials

For this session each student will need—
- the James 4 Scripture sheet
- the student journal page for Session 8
- his or her own Bible, pen, and notebook

You'll also need—
- a whiteboard and markers
- colored pencils (at least two colors per student)
- worship tools: a media experience with songs and Scripture (see Wrapping It Up)
- Large-Group Option: Create a video of you in your church sanctuary talking about how the busyness of ministry can rob you of true sanctuary time with God.

2. Session Intro

GOALS OF SESSION 8
As students experience this session, they will—
- explore the connection between sanctuary time with God and strength to beat temptation.
- discover the benefits of obeying God's instructions.
- practice creating a sanctuary experience with the group.

PRAYER

OPEN: *BUT IT'S A "GOOD BUSY"*
Group Interaction: Discuss the idea that if Satan can't get you to sin, he'll get you busy.

3. Digging In: *We've Got a Few Problems Here*

Group Dig: Explore James 4:1-12 to see what kind of problems James' readers were experiencing.

4. Cross-Checking: *Then You Walked into the Sanctuary*

Group Dig: Students will see that even Hebrew priests were tempted if they didn't get their time with God.
Large-Group Option: Before your session, create a video about your personal busyness.

5. Taking It Inward: *Let's Hear It for Asaph!*

Group Interaction: What can Old Testament Asaph and New Testament James teach a 21st century student about following God?

6. Wrapping It Up: *Finding Your Own Sanctuary*

Sanctuary Options: Choose an option that will help your students begin experiencing the strength and power of true sanctuary time with God.

1. Materials

For this session each student will need—
- the James 4 Scripture sheet
- the student journal page for Session 8
- his or her own Bible, pen, and notebook

You'll also need—
- a whiteboard and markers
- colored pencils (at least three colors per student)
- worship tools: a media experience with songs and Scripture (see Wrapping It Up)

2. Session Intro

GOALS OF SESSION 8

As students experience this session, they will—
- explore the connection between sanctuary time with God and strength to beat temptation.
- discover the benefits of obeying God's instructions.
- practice creating a sanctuary experience with the group.

PRAYER

OPEN: *BUT IT'S A "GOOD BUSY"*
Group Interaction: Discuss the idea that if Satan can't get you to sin, he'll get you busy.

3. Digging In: *We've Got a Few Problems Here*

Group Dig: Explore James 4:1-12 to see what kind of problems James' readers were experiencing.

4. Cross-Checking: *Then You Walked into the Sanctuary*

Personal Retreat: Students will see that even Hebrew priests were tempted if they didn't get their time with God.

5. Taking It Inward: *Let's Hear It for Asaph!*

Group Interaction: What can Old Testament Asaph and New Testament James teach a 21st century student about following God?

6. Wrapping It Up: *Finding Your Own Sanctuary*

Sanctuary Options: Choose an option that will help your students begin experiencing the strength and power of true sanctuary time with God.

JAMES 4:1-12
SANCTUARY

1. Materials

For this session each student will need—
- the James 4 Scripture sheet
- the student journal page for Session 8
- his or her own Bible, pen, and notebook

You'll also need—
- a whiteboard and markers
- colored pencils (at least two colors per student)
- worship tools: a media experience with songs and Scripture (see Wrapping It Up)

2. Session Intro

GOALS OF SESSION 8
As students experience this session, they will—
- explore the connection between sanctuary time with God and strength to beat temptation.
- discover the benefits of obeying God's instructions.
- practice creating a sanctuary experience with the group.

PRAYER

OPEN: *BUT IT'S A "GOOD BUSY"*
Group Interaction: Discuss the idea that if Satan can't get you to sin, he'll get you busy.

3. Digging In: *We've Got a Few Problems Here*

Group Dig: Explore James 4:1-12 to see what kind of problems James' readers were experiencing.

4. Cross-Checking: *Then You Walked into the Sanctuary*

Personal Retreat: Students will see that even Hebrew priests were tempted if they didn't get their time with God.

5. Taking It Inward: *Let's Hear It for Asaph!*

Group Interaction: What can Old Testament Asaph and New Testament James teach a 21st century student about following God?

6. Wrapping It Up: *Finding Your Own Sanctuary*

Sanctuary Options: Choose an option that will help your students begin experiencing the strength and power of true sanctuary time with God.

OUTLINE **COFFEEHOUSE** SESSION 8

1. Materials

For this session each student will need—
- his or her own Bible and pen
- optional: journal pages for Session 8 (Using the student journal page is optional in the coffeehouse setting because table space may be limited.)

You'll also need—
- a pack of pencils with erasers
- optional: a few spare Bibles for students who've forgotten theirs

2. Session Intro

GOALS OF SESSION 8

As students experience this session, they will—
- explore the connection between sanctuary time with God and strength to beat temptation.
- discover the benefits of obeying God's instructions.
- be challenged to create personal sanctuary time with God.

PRAYER

OPEN: *BUT IT'S A "GOOD BUSY"*
Group Interaction: Discuss the idea that if Satan can't get you to sin, he'll get you busy.

3. Digging In: *We've Got a Few Problems Here*

Group Dig: Explore James 4:1-12 to see what kind of problems James' readers were experiencing.

4. Cross-Checking: *Then You Walked into the Sanctuary*

Group Dig: Students will see that even Hebrew priests were tempted if they didn't get their time with God.

5. Taking It Inward: *Let's Hear It for Asaph!*

Group Interaction: What can Old Testament Asaph and New Testament James teach a 21st century student about following God?

6. Wrapping It Up: *Finding Your Own Sanctuary*

Sanctuary Options: Discuss some practical ways to experience the promises God gives in James. Students may take the optional journal pages home to use as a guide in establishing sanctuary time with God.

1. Materials (Optional)

- The opening song/credits of any episode of the TV sitcom *Friends*. Another option would be to find the lyrics of the song online and project them on a screen while the theme song, "I'll Be There for You," recorded by The Rembrandts, plays.

2. Optional Openings

Video Clip: Show or play the video/audio of the opening theme song from the TV sitcom *Friends*.

Quotations: Share a few quotations to introduce the idea of drawing near to God.

3. Digging In

Personal Story: Share a story about a relationship with a friend who keeps you accountable and encourages you in your faith.

4. Digging Deeper

James 4:1-10

5. Taking It Inward

Personal Story: Continue your personal story by explaining how your accountability friendship has improved your relationship with Christ.

6. Wrapping It Up

Challenge students to find time to draw near to God within the next 48 hours.

Setting the Heart

> My frame was not hidden from you when I was made in the secret place. When I was woven together in the depths of the earth, your eyes saw my unformed body. All the days ordained for me were written in your book before one of them came to be. (Psalm 139:15-16)

God ordained all of your days—even before the day of your conception. That means he chose your ordained days to be now, at this particular point in history. Have you ever noticed how certain people have used their precise time in history to great advantage? For example, would we recognize the name Beethoven if he'd been born before the invention of the piano? Or Michael Jordan before the birth of basketball? Or Bill Gates before the integrated circuit?

Is it possible that you were meant to use your ordained days to similar advantage? Let that question bounce around in your mind as you study what James—and ultimately God—has to say on the subject.

Digging In

Watching Time Go By

Under some conditions life seems short. At other times life seems long. Under all conditions life is limited. We've each received a set number of days at a particular point in history. And we've each been given an opportunity to observe God's creation during a short span of what we know as time.

In chapter 4, James makes a quick detour from his previous subject and gives a brief discourse on the subject of time. It's just five verses, but James is emphatic about what he says. In fact, he introduces the subject with, "Now listen." We should!

Read James 4:13-17 using your Scripture sheets. As you read—

1. Draw a clock ![clock] over every reference to time.

2. Underline any references to life.

After you've read and marked the passage, answer the following questions:

What does the passage teach us about *tomorrow*?

What does it teach us about *life?*

What instruction does James give to teach us what to do with the time we've been given?

Taking It Inward

To Plan or Not to Plan?

James describes life as a mist that appears and vanishes (4:14). Think about your life as a mist for a moment. Compare the way you plan your life with James' examples. Are you more like the person described in verse 13 or the one in verse 15?

If you're more like Mr. or Ms. James 4:13, do you boast or brag about your plans today or tomorrow? If you're thinking, *Nah, I'd never do that*, consider how you communicate your goals or vision for ministry. Do you confidently state these things in a way that presupposes what God is going to do?

Cross-Checking

Jesus on Time

It's worth our time to check out Jesus' teaching on life and how to use it. Read Luke 12:22-31 from your Bible.

What does Jesus tell us not to worry about?

What does he tell us to worry about? (key word: seek)

What parallels can you draw between *knowing the good you ought to do* in James 4:17 and *seeking his kingdom* in Luke 12:31?

Some people get guilt-trip chills down their spines when they hear the phrase *sins of omission*. They may be tempted to rationalize the guilt away: *I can't be held responsible for all the good I might have done but didn't.* But Scripture says otherwise. As you read the following passages, record what you learn about not doing the good you're supposed to do.

Proverbs 3:27-28

Matthew 7:26-27

Matthew 25:41-46

Luke 12:42-48

Insight

The Peril of Presuming

James touches on one specific sin in a backhanded way. Only the High School 2 and College Age sessions will touch on this sin. But even if you're not leading from one of those guides, you'll benefit from this background study.

SINS OF PRESUMPTION

The sin of presumption weaves its way through the entire Bible. What is this little-known sin? It's when we presume to know what God will say or do—when in reality, we don't know. We dabble in this sin when we assert what God prefers in such things as worship style, vision of ministry, and God's will about many matters he has not specifically addressed in his Word. This may make more sense when you read a few examples in Scripture. (Is it a coincidence that in the Bible, it was the spiritual leaders who were most susceptible to sins of presumption?) If you have Internet access, you may want to check out different Bible versions at www.Biblegateway.com.

Numbers 14:42-45

Deuteronomy 18:20

Psalm 19:13

1 Peter 4:11

Take a minute to journal your thoughts (or perhaps write a prayer) regarding two possible responses to the sin of presumption:

Is there anything for which you need to repent or ask forgiveness? If so, what?

Would you like to make a commitment similar to David's in Psalm 19:13?

Taking It Inward

Clear the Deck for Spontaneous Good!

Back to James 4:13-17. Let's see if these five little verses can help us make better use of the time we've been given.

First, a couple of facts:

> Your life is a mist.

> The mist appears for a little while and then vanishes.

Next a couple of questions:

> What did James say to do in the brief time in which your misty life exists?

> Look back at Luke 12:31. What did Jesus say to do in the brief time you've been given?

Now for the hard stuff—

> Are you willing to submit your calendar, your checkbook, your priorities, and your pursuits to the phrase, "If it is the Lord's will" (James 4:15)?

Are you willing to live by the phrase, "I don't even know what will happen tomorrow" (James 4:14) if it means loosening your grip on things that give you security and comfort? If your answer is yes, in what areas do you need to loosen your grip?

How can you adjust your schedule to allow for spontaneous good—the good you know you ought to do but rarely have time for?

Wrapping It Up

Seize the Day!

Why wait until you're with your students to begin applying James 4:13-17? Think about the good thing you ought to do. Now do it. Before today is over. (Remember, your life is a mist.)

After you've done the good things that came to mind, take a minute to select the appropriate Teach It guide for your session. (Full Teach It guides are on the CD-ROM accompanying this book.) Then read through the guide so you're familiar with the flow of the session and confident with each exercise. Be sure to allow time for printing or photocopying the Scripture sheets and student journal pages, and pulling together any materials needed.

Before you close your book, spend a moment praying for your group and your Bible study session. You're now several weeks into the material, so pray that students will stay motivated to experience all that God wants them to learn from his Word.

WEB SUPPORT:
Don't forget to check out Web support for *Hear and Do* at www.inword.org. You'll find updated media suggestions such as music and video clips along with more prep helps and specific application ideas. Look for the Digging Deeper series icon. You'll find password information in the Instructions at the front of this book.

1. Materials

For this session each student will need—
- the James 4 Scripture sheet
- the student journal page for Session 9
- his or her own Bible, pen, and notebook

You'll also need—
- a whiteboard and markers
- colored pencils (at least two colors per student)

2. Session Intro

GOALS OF SESSION 9

As students experience this session, they will—
- explore what James says about our time on earth.
- explore what Jesus says to do with our time on earth.
- be challenged to maximize their time on earth.

PRAYER

OPEN: *LIFE SPAN*
Group Interaction: Have students create a time line of their lives.

3. Digging In: *Watching Time Go By*

Group Dig: Explore James 4:13-17 to see what God has to say about our time on earth.

4. Cross-Checking: *Jesus on Time*

Personal Retreat: Explore some passages that tell us what Jesus has to say about our time on earth.

5. Taking It Inward: *Clear the Deck for Spontaneous Good*

Group Interaction: Process with each other what Jesus' teachings about time can look like in your typical day.

6. Wrapping It Up: *Seize the Day!*

Group Interaction: There's no time like now to start living out commitments from this session.

1. Materials

For this session each student will need—
- the James 4 Scripture sheet
- the student journal page for Session 9
- his or her own Bible, pen, and notebook

You'll also need—
- colored pencils (at least two colors per student)
- a long sheet of paper for a time line; you can use a whiteboard if paper isn't practical for your meeting space
- three or four markers to write on the sheet of paper
- life span trivia

2. Session Intro

GOALS OF SESSION 9

As students experience this session, they will—
- explore what James says about our time on earth.
- explore what Jesus says to do with our time on earth.
- be challenged to maximize their time on earth.

PRAYER

OPEN: *LIFE SPAN*
Group Interaction: Have students create a time line of their lives.
Group Interaction: Share some trivia about life spans.

3. Digging In: *Watching Time Go By*

Group Dig: Explore James 4:13-17 to see what God has to say about our time on earth.

4. Cross-Checking: *Jesus on Time*

Personal Retreat: Explore some passages that tell us what Jesus has to say about our time on earth.

5. Taking It Inward: *Clear the Deck for Spontaneous Good*

Group Interaction: Process with each other what Jesus' teachings about time can look like in your typical day.

6. Wrapping It Up: *Seize the Day!*

Group Interaction: There's no time like now to start living out commitments from this session.

1. Materials

For this session each student will need—
- the James 4 Scripture sheet
- the student journal page for Session 9
- his or her own Bible, pen, and notebook

You'll also need—
- a whiteboard and markers
- colored pencils (at least two colors per student)
- life span trivia

2. Session Intro

GOALS OF SESSION 9
As students experience this session, they will—
- explore what James says about our time on earth.
- explore what Jesus says to do with our time on earth.
- be challenged to maximize their time on earth.

PRAYER

OPEN: *LIFE SPAN*
Group Interaction: Share some trivia about life spans.

3. Digging In: *Watching Time Go By*

Group Dig: Explore James 4:13-17 to see what God has to say about our time on earth.

4. Cross-Checking: *Jesus on Time*

Personal Retreat: Explore some passages that tell us what Jesus has to say about our time on earth.

5. Taking It Inward: *Clear the Deck for Spontaneous Good*

Group Interaction: Process with each other what Jesus' teachings about time can look like in your typical day.

6. Digging Deeper: *Playing God*

Group Interaction: Discover why presumptuousness toward God is labeled a sin.

7. Wrapping It Up: *Seize the Day!*

Group Interaction: There's no time like now to start living out commitments from this session.

1. Materials

For this session each student will need—
- the James 4 Scripture sheet
- the student journal page for Session 9
- his or her own Bible, pen, and notebook

You'll also need—
- a whiteboard and markers
- colored pencils (at least two colors per student)
- life span trivia

2. Session Intro

GOALS OF SESSION 9

As students experience this session, they will—
- explore what James says about our time on earth.
- explore what Jesus says to do with our time on earth.
- be challenged to maximize their time on earth.

PRAYER

OPEN: *LIFE SPAN*

Group Interaction: Share some trivia about life spans.

3. Digging In: *Watching Time Go By*

Group Dig: Explore James 4:13-17 to see what God has to say about our time on earth.

4. Cross-Checking: *Jesus on Time*

Personal Retreat: Explore some passages that tell us what Jesus has to say about our time on earth.

5. Taking It Inward: *Clear the Deck for Spontaneous Good*

Group Interaction: Process with each other what Jesus' teachings about time can look like in your typical day.

6. Digging Deeper: *Playing God*

Group Interaction: Discover why presumptuousness toward God is labeled a sin.

7. Wrapping It Up: *Seize the Day!*

Group Interaction: There's no time like now to start living out commitments from this session.

1. Materials

For this session each student will need—
- his or her own Bible and pen
- optional: journal page for Session 9 (Using the student journal page is optional in the coffeehouse setting because table space may be limited.)

You'll also need—
- a pack of pencils with erasers
- optional: a few spare Bibles for students who've forgotten theirs
- life span trivia

2. Session Intro

GOALS OF SESSION 9
As students experience this session, they will—
- explore what James says about our time on earth.
- explore what Jesus says to do with our time on earth.
- be challenged to maximize their time on earth.

PRAYER

OPEN: *LIFE SPAN*
Group Interaction: Share some trivia about life spans.

3. Digging In: *Watching Time Go By*

Group Dig: Explore James 4:13-17 to see what God has to say about our time on earth.

4. Cross-Checking: *Jesus on Time*

Group Dig: Explore some passages that tell us what Jesus has to say about our time on earth.

5. Taking It Inward: *Clear the Deck for Spontaneous Good*

Group Interaction: Process with each other what Jesus' teachings about time can look like in your typical day.

6. Wrapping It Up: *Seize the Day!*

Group Interaction: There's no time like now to start living out commitments from this session.

1. Materials (Optional)

- A simple poster (or a more involved media presentation) depicting a graph of your lifetime and a speculative look at the rest of your life
- The song "Life Means So Much" by Chris Rice (you may want to print a lyric sheet or project lyric slides)

2. Optional Openings

Personal Time Line: Begin by showing a time line of your life. This can be as simple as a sketch on a piece of poster board or as complex as a media presentation.
Quotations: Share a few quotations about time.

3. Digging In

Personal Story: Share a personal illustration of how easy it is to get self-centered in our prayers. James 4:13-17

4. Taking It Inward

Find out what God is doing and join him, instead of asking God to join what you're doing.

5. Wrapping It Up

Ephesians 3:20-21: If God is able to do immeasurably more than what *we* ask, and he is, let's ask what *he* wants.

Setting the Heart

Money is one of the top five topics addressed in Scripture, receiving almost as much attention as the subject of love. But when you read carefully what God says about money, you'll see that money itself is not the problem. It's the *effect* of money. Some of the godliest people in Scripture—Job and Abraham, to name two—had immense wealth, even by the world's standards.

The problem is that the world's wealth can make us less dependent on God, who is the Source of all we have in the first place. Read the words God spoke through Moses just before his people entered the Promised Land:

> When the LORD your God brings you into the land he swore to your fathers, to Abraham, Isaac and Jacob, to give you—a land with large, flourishing cities you did not build, houses filled with all kinds of good things you did not provide, wells you did not dig, and vineyards and olive groves you did not plant—then when you eat and are satisfied, be careful that you do not forget the LORD, who brought you out of Egypt, out of the land of slavery... Be sure to keep the commands of the LORD your God and the stipulations and decrees he has given you. (Deuteronomy 6:10-12, 17)

The Lord desires that our behavior be driven by dependence on him. He trusts his Word—his commands, stipulations, and decrees—to keep us dependent. Perhaps we should trust it, too. James 5 is a great place to start.

Digging In

Getting the Big Picture

Read James 5:1-11 using your Scripture sheets. As you read—

1. Circle every reference to the readers of the letter.

2. In a different color, underline every reference to the Lord.

After you've read and marked the passage, review what you've underlined and list what you learn about the Lord. You'll notice that James uses the title "Lord" for both Jesus and God. Try to distinguish between the Lord Jesus and the Lord God as you make your list.

As you've studied the book of James, you may have noticed that James often refers to his readers as his brothers. In James 5:1 what group of people is he singling out?

James reserves some of his best word pictures for his warnings to the rich. Read James 5:1-6 again. Draw a box around the word pictures he uses to depict the situation of the rich. List these word pictures here.

In light of the fact that the Lord's coming is near, James encourages his readers to have a particular attitude. Read James 5:7-11 again. Record the instructions concerning this attitude.

Insight

Murder?!

James accused the rich of a pretty intense action toward the poor in verse 6—murder. Commentators speculate he was referring to the result of the rich cheating the poor out of their only means of income—their land. Without livelihood or sustenance, the poor literally starved to death.

Digging Deeper

Harsh Words for the Rich

So, who were these rich people in James 5? At first glance, you might assume James was addressing the rich who were part of the Christian community he was writing to—the twelve tribes scattered among the nations. Many scholars believe these rich people were outside the Christian community and that James was warning them in defense of his primary audience. (In James 2:5-7 we learned that James' readers were being exploited by the rich.)

The wording of James 5:7—"Be patient, then, brothers"—seems to reflect a return to James' original audience: the Christian community. If this is the case, then James 5:7-11 is powerful encouragement for those being oppressed by the rich. This conclusion is supported by James' many references to perseverance in other parts of his letter.

Whether the rich in James 5 were within the Christian community or not, one thing is clear: their actions against the poor were wrong—a recurring theme throughout the letter. Take a minute to revisit the following verses. Jot down what you learn about the rich and the poor.

James 1:9-11

James 2:1-5

James 4:13-14

What's the common theme in these passages?

Which group of people is commonly on the receiving end of James' instructions?

Cross-Checking

What's Your Account Balance? (Does It Even Matter?)

James' strong language toward the rich indicates God doesn't have much patience with the self-indulgent or those who hoard treasure. With God it's not the amount of wealth that's the problem, but how the money is obtained and what's done with it after it's accumulated.

As you read these passages, note what you learn about the behavior God desires.

Exodus 23:9

Psalm 82:1-4

Micah 6:8

Matthew 5:7

Luke 6:31-36

Romans 13:7-8

Taking It Inward

Share the Wealth

Review the instructions from James 5:7-11 that you listed under Digging In. How would you characterize the type of behavior we should have?

As you've probably noticed, James 5:1-11 consists of two segments—warnings to the rich and instructions for behavior. (The little word *then* in verse 7 ties these segments together.) Both of these segments are to be understood in light of the fact that Jesus' coming is near. So, we have at least two good ways to apply this passage: as words of warning and as words of hope.

WORDS OF WARNING

You can be rich without having money. You can be rich in personality, intelligence, leadership, initiative, and so on. And when we interact with people who aren't as rich as we are—in whatever area—our first impulse is often impatience. This may explain why James follows his assessment of the rich with admonitions of patience.

In which of the following areas do you consider yourself rich?

☐ friendships   ☐ self-motivation

☐ decisiveness   ☐ enthusiasm

☐ common sense   ☐ vision

☐ planning   ☐ personality

☐ intelligence   ☐ physical skill

☐ organization   ☐ problem solving

☐ other _____

How do you tend to react to those who are deficient in the areas where you're rich? If it's negatively, in what ways can your reaction have an oppressive effect on those people?

What can you do to share your riches?

What can you do to extend your patience?

What can you do to avoid grumbling?

WORDS OF HOPE

James dealt with perseverance through trials in the first chapter and now returns to it in the last chapter. If you've been doing this study at a rate of one session per week, it's been eight weeks since you studied James 1. You may be experiencing a completely different set of trials by now.

What circumstances are weighing heavily on your heart?

What situations are you or your friends experiencing that seem hopeless?

How's work? Do you feel exploited or oppressed?

One of the most awesome themes of the New Testament is hope—specifically, the hope that no matter how tough this life may get, Jesus is coming back. Until his return, his grace and mercy—administered by the Holy Spirit—will comfort, restore, and preserve us. As you read the following passages, note the attitudes and actions we should have in light of his imminent return. Take time to apply these to any of the situations you just listed.

1 Corinthians 1:7-9

Philippians 4:4-6

1 Thessalonians 5:22-23

Hebrews 10:23-25

Hebrews 10:34-37

Revelation 22:20-21

Wrapping It Up

Make a Prayer Deposit

Believers will experience heaven—either when they die or when Jesus returns. And either of these events could happen sooner than we think. Before you meet with your students, give the Spirit an opportunity to impress upon you the reality of heaven and the certainty of Christ's return. Trust the words of James, and let your behavior reflect your dependence on God rather than on the wealth of this world.

Before you close your book, select the appropriate Teach It guide for your session. (Full Teach It guides are on the CD-ROM accompanying this book.) Then read through the guide so you're familiar with the flow of the session and confident with each exercise. Be sure to allow time for printing or photocopying the Scripture sheets and student journal pages, and pulling together any materials needed.

Close your prep time by praying for your group session. Pray that your students will use this session to begin to develop a trust in God's Word as they learn they can depend on God's perspective.

WEB SUPPORT:
Don't forget to check out Web support for *Hear and Do* at www.inword.org. You'll find updated media suggestions such as music and video clips along with more prep helps and specific application ideas. Look for the Digging Deeper series icon. You'll find password information in the Instructions at the front of this book.

EXERCISE HEADS-UP
One of the Open options for the High School 2 guide of Session 10 will take a little legwork. You'll want to look at those instructions and prepare a few days ahead of time.

1. Materials

For this session each student will need—
- the James 5 Scripture sheet
- the student journal page for Session 10
- his or her own Bible, pen, and notebook

You'll also need—
- a whiteboard and markers
- colored pencils (at least two colors per student)
- a pack of play money from a dollar store or an old Monopoly game

2. Session Intro

GOALS OF SESSION 10

As students experience this session, they will—
- discover how treatment of the poor ranks with God.
- explore ways they are rich that have nothing to do with money.
- be challenged to adjust their priorities and pursuits according to a godly perspective.

PRAYER

OPEN: *THE GOOD AND BAD OF MONEY*

Group Interaction: Use play money to discuss the best and worst uses of money your students have ever heard of.

3. Digging In: *Painting the Money Picture*

Group Dig: Explore James 5:1-11 to see what you learn about the first readers of James' letter and about God regarding money matters.

4. Taking It Inward: *Harsh Words for the Rich*

Group Interaction: Students process James' warnings and help each other see how rich they are in areas that have nothing to do with money.

5. Cross-Checking: *What's Your Account Balance? (Does It Even Matter?)*

Personal Retreat: Students will explore one of the Bible's most talked-about subjects—the treatment of the poor by God's people.

6. Taking It Inward: *Share the Wealth*

Group Interaction: Students encourage each other to share out of their personal riches—whatever those riches might be—to help others.

7. Wrapping It Up: *Make a Prayer Deposit*

Personal Prayer: Spend the closing moments of the session in silent prayer, processing the fact that all James' instructions about money are accompanied by the hope that Jesus is coming back any minute.

JAMES 5:1-11
IT'S NOT JUST THE MONEY

1. Materials

For this session each student will need—
- the James 5 Scripture sheet
- the student journal page for Session 10
- his or her own Bible, pen, and notebook

You'll also need—
- a whiteboard and markers
- colored pencils (at least two colors per student)
- a $10 or $20 bill

2. Session Intro

GOALS OF SESSION 10
As students experience this session, they will—
- discover how treatment of the poor ranks with God.
- explore ways they are rich that have nothing to do with money.
- be challenged to adjust their priorities and pursuits according to a godly perspective.

PRAYER

OPEN: *THE GOOD AND BAD OF MONEY*
Group Interaction: Use a $10 or $20 bill to get your students thinking about how money can be used for good or for bad.

3. Digging In: *Painting the Money Picture*

Group Dig: Explore James 5:1-11 to see what you learn about the first readers of James' letter and about God regarding money matters.

4. Taking It Inward: *Harsh Words for the Rich*

Group Interaction: Students process James' warnings and help each other see how rich they are in areas that have nothing to do with money.

5. Cross-Checking: *What's Your Account Balance? (Does It Even Matter?)*

Personal Retreat: Students will explore one of the Bible's most talked-about subjects—the treatment of the poor by God's people.

6. Taking It Inward: *Share the Wealth!*

Group Interaction: Students encourage each other to share out of their personal riches—whatever those riches might be—to help others.

7. Wrapping It Up: *Make a Prayer Deposit*

Personal Prayer: Spend the closing moments of the session in silent prayer, processing the fact that all James' instructions about money are accompanied by the hope that Jesus is coming back any minute.

1. Materials

For this session each student will need—
- the James 5 Scripture sheet
- the student journal page for Session 10
- his or her own Bible, pen, and notebook

You'll also need—
- a whiteboard and markers
- colored pencils (at least two colors per student)
- optional: a $10 or $20 bill
- optional: a $50 or $100 bill that's out of circulation

2. Session Intro

GOALS OF SESSION 10
As students experience this session, they will—
- discover how treatment of the poor ranks with God.
- explore ways they are rich that have nothing to do with money.
- be challenged to adjust their priorities and pursuits according to a godly perspective.

PRAYER

OPEN: *THE GOOD AND BAD OF MONEY*
Group Option 1: Use a $10 or $20 bill to get your students thinking about how money can be used for good or for bad.
Group Option 2: Cut up an out-of-circulation $100 bill to get your students thinking about how the money could have been used.

3. Digging In: *Painting the Money Picture*

Group Dig: Explore James 5:1-11 to see what you learn about the first readers of James' letter and about God regarding money matters.

4. Digging Deeper: *Take It to the Bank*

Group Read: Look at some passages showing that God is not anti-wealth.

5. Taking It Inward: *Harsh Words for the Rich*

Group Interaction: Students process James' warnings and help each other see how rich they are in areas that have nothing to do with money.

6. Cross-Checking: *What's Your Account Balance? (Does It Even Matter?)*

Personal Retreat: Students will explore one of the Bible's most talked-about subjects—the treatment of the poor by God's people.

7. Taking It Inward: *Share the Wealth!*

Group Interaction: Students encourage each other to share out of their personal riches—whatever those riches might be—to help others.

8. Wrapping It Up: *Make a Prayer Deposit*

Personal Prayer: Spend the closing moments of the session in silent prayer, processing the fact that all James' instructions about money are accompanied by the hope that Jesus is coming back any minute.

1. Materials

For this session each student will need—
- the James 5 Scripture sheet
- the student journal page for Session 10
- his or her own Bible, pen, and notebook

You'll also need—
- a whiteboard and markers
- colored pencils (at least two colors per student)
- a $10 or $20 bill

2. Session Intro

GOALS OF SESSION 10

As students experience this session, they will—
- discover how treatment of the poor ranks with God.
- explore ways they are rich that have nothing to do with money.
- be challenged to adjust their priorities and pursuits according to a godly perspective.

PRAYER

OPEN: *THE GOOD AND BAD OF MONEY*
Group Interaction: Use a $10 or $20 bill to discuss the best and worst uses of money your students have ever heard of.

3. Digging In: *Painting the Money Picture*

Group Dig: Explore James 5:1-11 to see what you learn about the first readers of James' letter and about God regarding money matters.

4. Digging Deeper: *Take It to the Bank*

Group Read: Look at some passages showing that God is not anti-wealth.

5. Taking It Inward: *Harsh Words for the Rich*

Group Interaction: Students process James' warnings and help each other see how rich they are in areas that have nothing to do with money.

6. Cross-Checking: *What's Your Account Balance? (Does It Even Matter?)*

Personal Retreat: Students will explore one of the Bible's most talked-about subjects—the treatment of the poor by God's people.

7. Taking It Inward: *Share the Wealth!*

Group Interaction: Students encourage each other to share out of their personal riches—whatever those riches might be—to help others.

8. Wrapping It Up: *Make a Prayer Deposit*

Personal Prayer: Spend the closing moments of the session in silent prayer and processing the fact that all James' instructions about money are accompanied by the hope that Jesus is coming back any minute.

1. Materials

For this session each student will need—
- his or her own Bible and pen
- optional: journal page for Session 10 (Using the student journal page is optional in the coffeehouse setting because table space may be limited.)

You'll also need—
- a pack of pencils with erasers
- optional: a few spare Bibles for students who've forgotten theirs
- a $10 or $20 bill

2. Session Intro

GOALS OF SESSION 10

As students experience this session, they will—
- discover how treatment of the poor ranks with God.
- explore ways they are rich that have nothing to do with money.
- be challenged to adjust their priorities and pursuits according to a godly perspective.

PRAYER

OPEN: *THE GOOD AND BAD OF MONEY*

Group Interaction: Use a $10 or $20 bill to discuss the best and worst uses of money your students have ever heard of.

3. Digging In: *Painting the Money Picture*

Group Dig: Explore James 5:1-11 to see what you learn about the first readers of James' letter and about God regarding money matters.

4. Taking It Inward: *Harsh Words for the Rich*

Group Interaction: Students process James' warnings and help each other see how rich they are in areas that have nothing to do with money.

5. Cross-Checking: *What's Your Account Balance? (Does It Even Matter?)*

Group Dig: Students will explore one of the Bible's most talked-about subjects—the treatment of the poor by God's people.

6. Taking It Inward: *Share the Wealth!*

Group Interaction: Students encourage each other to share out of their personal riches—whatever those riches might be—to help others.

7. Wrapping It Up: *Walk-Out Challenge*

Group Interaction: Give students a *walk-out challenge* to, as they leave, dwell on Jesus' return.

1. Materials (Optional)

A student (one who doesn't mind hamming it up) to mock you as you begin your talk; or use a video clip of someone mocking a teacher behind his or her back.

2. Optional Openings

Visual Illustration: Have one of your students stand behind you and mock or mimic you as you begin your talk.

Quotations: Share some quotations to introduce the idea of what motivates us to do good things—seen or unseen, rewarded or unrewarded.

3. Digging In

Personal Story: Tell a personal story about a time when you did a random act of kindness or sacrificed for something that would bring you no tangible reward.

4. Digging Deeper

James 5:7-9

Optional Mix-Ins: A few facts you may want to point out about this passage in James.

Personal Illustration: Share a personal illustration about a time you had to wait and endure.

5. Taking It Inward

How would life be different if we could tangibly see Jesus right beside us?

6. Wrapping It Up

Challenge: What have you been thinking about all day? How would your thoughts be different if you knew they were the last thoughts you'd have before Jesus returned?

Setting the Heart

Here's something you've got to see:

> Very early in the morning, while it was still dark, Jesus got up, left the house and went off to a solitary place, where he prayed. (Mark 1:35)

> But Jesus often withdrew to lonely places and prayed. (Luke 5:16)

> One of those days Jesus went out to a mountainside to pray, and spent the night praying to God. (Luke 6:12)

> About eight days after Jesus said this, he took Peter, John and James with him and went up onto a mountain to pray. (Luke 9:28)

> One day Jesus was praying in a certain place. (Luke 11:1)

Jesus prayed early in the morning, throughout the night, by himself, with his friends, on a mountainside, in lonely places. And these are just a few of the times and places he prayed. Jesus couldn't wait to talk with the Father—anytime, anyplace.

Perhaps your prayer life has become haphazard—or even nonexistent. Today, let Jesus' example and James' teaching move you to become a person of prayer—anytime, anyplace.

Digging In

Everything You Wanted to Know about Prayer

Read James 5:12-18 using your Scripture sheets. As you read, circle every mention of prayer.

After you've finished, list every instruction concerning prayer.

Now list anything that gives insight into how you should pray. Look for things you're told to do, as well as descriptions of the intensity of prayer.

List the results of prayer that you find.

Insight

The Mysterious Land between Prayer and Healing

What about people we pray for who aren't healed? The session with your teens doesn't specifically cover this topic, but they may ask the question. To help you prepare for the group discussion, here are some points to consider as you study James 5.

THROUGHOUT SCRIPTURE, SOME SICKNESSES WENT UNHEALED.
Paul prayed three times for his thorn in the flesh (possibly a physical ailment) to be removed. Paul was righteous and his prayer was fervent, yet the thorn was not removed (2 Corinthians 12:7-10).

In 2 Timothy 4:20 Paul left his coworker, Trophimus, sick. Certainly Paul and the apostles, prayer warriors all, would have prayed for his healing, yet Trophimus' illness disrupted his ministry with Paul.

In many Scriptures, including James 1, we're told that sicknesses and hardships will come. Yet believers are encouraged to endure these trials, not expect them to always be removed.

THE PHRASE *OFFERED IN FAITH* IS OFTEN MISUNDERSTOOD.
To offer a prayer in faith isn't the same as saying, "I really, really believe God's going to heal." The phrase offered in faith parallels Jesus' instruction to pray in his name and receive what we ask (see John 14:13; 15:16; 16:23). To pray in Jesus' name is to pray a prayer Jesus would pray. Thus the prayer offered in faith is a prayer in accordance with God's will.

God can heal anyone at any time. When we offer our prayer in faith, we are submitting to God's sovereign will with the full knowledge that he can heal, but that his ways and plans are higher than ours (Isaiah 55:9). The true prayer of faith joins Shadrach, Meshach, and Abednego in declaring, "The God we serve is able to save and rescue us. But even if he doesn't, our trust is in him alone!" (Daniel 3:17-18, paraphrased).

The phrase **will make the sick person well** may seem more definitive than it really is.

James' promise that the prayer offered in faith will make the sick person well doesn't leave much wiggle room for those who aren't made well. But even here there are some factors worth looking at.

First, the last half of this verse tells us how the sick person will be made well: the Lord will raise him up, and if he has sinned, he will be forgiven. This seems to point to a spiritual aspect of the healing, and in fact, the Greek word used here (*sozo*) can be translated *saved* or *healed*.

Second, we're not given a clue as to the timing of the healing. It could be immediately after the prayer, at the time of Jesus' return, or after death.

The bottom line is we can't manipulate God. Perhaps the best way to understand this challenging passage is to focus on our part of the prayer process—and leave the results up to God.

Taking It Inward

Shall We Pray?

On that note, let's assume the most beneficial way to experience this passage is simply to do it—follow the steps and apply the actions James gave us, focusing on our responsibility in the prayer process.

WHAT WE SHOULD PRAY FOR

You listed situations we should pray about when you studied James 5:12-18. Now list anyone around you who falls into one of these categories—or anything you're personally experiencing that fits these descriptions.

START WITH YOURSELF

James hints that effective prayer begins with the inner life. Find the hints about our internal spiritual health in James 5:16, and write them here.

Has it ever occurred to you that an atmosphere of repentance and confession is the atmosphere most conducive to the mighty work of God? The great revivals of history ignited when God's people confessed and repented of their sins. Maybe God is waiting for that kind of atmosphere to be unleashed in your student ministry or church. And perhaps it could begin with you.

Spend some time studying the following Bible verses. Look for the benefits of confession, as well as any consequences of not confessing our sins.

2 Chronicles 7:13-15

Psalm 51:1-10

Psalm 66:16-20

Proverbs 28:13-14

1 John 1:9-10

What do you need to confess? Write it in code if someone else will be reading this. Don't stop there. Carefully reread James 5:16, looking for what else (or whom else) your confession should involve.

SHOW GOD YOU'RE SERIOUS
What are the practical steps James 5:12-18 gives to those preparing to offer a prayer in faith?

What are some ways your group or student ministry can apply the instruction to call the elders to pray?

If your church doesn't have designated elders or if your student ministry functions apart from a local church, how can you still apply the principles given in James? Remember, taking the Lord's instructions at face value shows him we're serious about obedience. Pray about what he would have your group do, then jot down your impressions.

ADOPT THE INTENSITY

In verses 16 and 17 James gives a couple of clues about the level of prayer intensity God is looking for. Find these and write them down.

What needs to change in your prayer life so it looks like the life of prayer James describes in these verses? Over the next two days, what can you give up, cancel, or reschedule to free up a block of time for earnest prayer?

Wrapping It Up

Light the Fire

Take God at his Word. Between now and the group session, dedicate yourself to praying the way James exhorts us to pray. Perhaps you and your students are to be the catalyst for establishing an atmosphere of physical and spiritual healing in your church or ministry. It all can start with you.

Before you close your book, select the appropriate Teach It guide for your session. (Full Teach It guides are on the CD-ROM accompanying this book.). Then read through the guide so you're familiar with the flow of the session and confident with each exercise. Be sure to allow time for printing or photocopying the Scripture sheets and student journal pages, and pulling together any materials needed.

Take a moment to pray for your students and your group session. Let the subject matter of this session marinate in your mind while you think about the issues your students are facing. Trust God's Spirit to make the connection between God's Word and your student's needs.

WEB SUPPORT:
Web support for *Hear and Do* is available at www.inword.org. Since you're nearing the close of this study, check out the long-term follow-up ideas to help your students keep their experience in James fresh. You'll find password information in the Instructions at the front of this book.

EXERCISE HEADS-UP

The structure of this session is somewhat different from other sessions. It contains options that require some prior thought and preparation. You may want to read through the session now. You may also want to confer with your pastor about any doctrines or beliefs held by your church or denomination that should be taught in this session.

1. Materials

For this session each student will need—
- the James 5 Scripture sheet
- the student journal page for Session 11
- his or her own Bible, pen, and notebook

You'll also need—
- a whiteboard and markers
- colored pencils (at least one color per student)
- optional: anointing oil

2. Session Intro

GOALS OF SESSION 11
As students experience this session, they will—
- explore Jesus' examples and James' teaching on prayer.
- be introduced to the confession side of prayer.
- be challenged to become a person of prayer.

OPEN: *HIDE AND SEEK*
Group Interaction: Start this session with *Hide and Seek*, either discussing it or playing it.

PRAYER

3. Digging In: *Everything You Wanted to Know about Prayer*

Group Dig: Explore James 5:12-18 to see what this short passage has to say about prayer.

4. Taking It Inward: *Shall We Pray?*

Group Share: Process together the different areas of prayer James addresses.

5. Cross-Checking: *The Great 10-Minute Bible Study on Prayer*

Group Dig: Help students apply scriptural models of prayer to their personal prayer lives.

6. Wrapping It Up: *Light the Fire*

Group Interaction: From singing songs of praise to making the first entry in a prayer journal, choose the prayer option that best fits your group.

JAMES 5:12-18
LET'S DO PRAYER

1. Materials

For this session each student will need—
- the James 5 Scripture sheet
- the student journal page for Session 11
- his or her own Bible, pen, and notebook

You'll also need—
- a whiteboard and markers
- colored pencils (at least one color per student)
- optional: anointing oil

2. Session Intro

GOALS OF SESSION 11
As students experience this session, they will—
- explore Jesus' examples and James' teaching on prayer.
- be introduced to the confession side of prayer.
- be challenged to become a person of prayer.

PRAYER

OPEN: *HIDE AND SEEK*
Group Interaction: Start this session by asking students to discuss their last game of *Hide and Seek*.

3. Digging In: *Everything You Wanted to Know about Prayer*

Group Dig: Explore James 5:12-18 to see what this short passage has to say about prayer.

4. Taking It Inward: *Shall We Pray?*

Group Share: Process together the different areas of prayer James addresses.

5. Cross-Checking: *The Great 10-Minute Bible Study on Prayer*

Group Dig: Help students apply scriptural models of prayer to their personal prayer lives.

6. Wrapping It Up: *Light the Fire*

Group Interaction: From singing songs of praise to making the first entry in a prayer journal, choose the prayer option that best fits your group.

JAMES 5:12-18
LET'S DO PRAYER

1. Materials

For this session each student will need—
- the James 5 Scripture sheet
- the student journal page for Session 11
- his or her own Bible, pen, and notebook

You'll also need—
- a whiteboard and markers
- colored pencils (at least one color per student)
- optional: anointing oil

2. Session Intro

GOALS OF SESSION 11

As students experience this session, they will—
- explore Jesus' examples and James' teaching on prayer.
- be introduced to the confession side of prayer.
- be challenged to become a person of prayer.

PRAYER

OPEN: *PRAY THE JESUS WAY*

Group Interaction: Start this session by showing students the different times and places Jesus prayed.

3. Digging In: *Everything You Wanted to Know about Prayer*

Group Dig: Explore James 5:12-18 to see what this short passage has to say about prayer.

4. Taking It Inward: *Shall We Pray?*

Group Share: Process together the different areas of prayer James addresses.

5. Cross-Checking: *The Great 10-Minute Bible Study on Prayer*

Personal Retreat: Help students apply scriptural models of prayer to their personal prayer lives.

6. Wrapping It Up: *Light the Fire*

Group Interaction: From singing songs of praise to making the first entry in a prayer journal, choose the prayer option that best fits your group.

JAMES 5:12-18
LET'S DO PRAYER

1. Materials

For this session each student will need—
- the James 5 Scripture sheet
- the student journal page for Session 11
- his or her own Bible, pen, and notebook

You'll also need—
- a whiteboard and markers
- colored pencils (at least one color per student)
- optional: anointing oil

2. Session Intro

GOALS OF SESSION 11
As students experience this session, they will—
- explore Jesus' examples and James' teaching on prayer.
- be introduced to the confession side of prayer.
- be challenged to become a person of prayer.

OPEN: *PRAY THE JESUS WAY*
Group Interaction: Start this session by showing students the different times and places Jesus prayed.

PRAYER

3. Digging In: *Everything You Wanted to Know about Prayer*
Group Dig: Explore James 5:12-18 to see what this short passage has to say about prayer.

4. Taking It Inward: *Shall We Pray?*
Group Share: Process together the different areas of prayer James addresses.

5. Cross-Checking: *The Great 10-Minute Bible Study on Prayer*

Personal Retreat: Help students apply scriptural models of prayer to their personal prayer lives.

6. Wrapping It Up: *Light the Fire*

Group Interaction: From singing songs of praise to making the first entry in a prayer journal, choose the prayer option that best fits your group.

1. Materials

For this session each student will need—
- his or her own Bible and pen
- optional: journal page for Session 11 (Using the student journal page is optional in the coffeehouse setting because table space may be limited.)

You'll also need—
- a pack of pencils with erasers
- optional: a few spare Bibles for students who've forgotten theirs
- anointing oil

2. Session Intro

GOALS OF SESSION 11
As students experience this session, they will—
- explore Jesus' examples and James' teaching on prayer.
- be introduced to the confession side of prayer.
- be challenged to become a person of prayer.

OPEN: *PRAY THE JESUS WAY*
Group Interaction: Start this session by showing students the different times and places Jesus prayed.

PRAYER

3. Digging In: *Everything You Wanted to Know about Prayer*

Group Dig: Explore James 5:12-18 to see what this short passage has to say about prayer.

4. Taking It Inward: *Shall We Pray?*

Group Share: Process together the different areas of prayer James addresses.

5. Cross-Checking: *The Great 10-Minute Bible Study on Prayer*
Group Dig: Help students apply scriptural models of prayer to their personal prayer lives.

6. Wrapping It Up: *Light the Fire*
Group Interaction: Find a time to begin applying James' prayer model.

JAMES 5:12-18
LET'S DO PRAYER

1. Materials (Optional)

A cell phone with speakerphone; create a few words to be used for a word guessing game.

2. Optional Openings

Group Interaction: Ask for a volunteer to play *Catch Phrase* over the phone.
Quotations: Share some quotations to introduce the importance of prayer.

3. Digging In

Personal Story: Share a personal story that illustrates prayer being taken seriously.

4. Digging Deeper

James 5:12-18

5. Taking It Inward

We're willing to seek God from many sources. Why not try God himself?

6. Wrapping It Up

Prayer shows that we admit God knows more than we do.

SESSION 12

JAMES 5:19-20
TOTAL TURNAROUND

Setting the Heart

The Sadducees were a Jewish sect prominent in Jesus' day who didn't believe in Jesus' resurrection, or life after death. Knowing that Jesus wasn't just claiming to be the Son of God, but also trumpeting the promise of eternal life, the Sadducees felt threatened. They figured if they could embarrass Jesus and unravel his claims by throwing him a stumper question in front of a large crowd, they'd never hear from him again. So they pulled together their brightest minds and presented their most airtight, faith-unraveling question (about marriage in heaven). Read in the following passage how Jesus began his response, along with the reaction of the awestruck crowd.

> Jesus replied, "You are in error because you do not know the Scriptures or the power of God." When the crowds heard this, they were astonished at his teaching. (Matthew 22:29, 33)

The Sadducees failed to accomplish their mission—and Jesus nailed the reason for their error. Are we, today, different from the Sadducees? Even among believers, plans fail, energy is wasted, and misguided decisions are made because people know neither the Scriptures nor the power of God.

Scholar Douglas J. Moo, in *The Letter of James (The Pillar New Testament Commentary,* 2000), asserts the book of James contains more imperatives (direct commands and instructions) per word than any other New Testament book. It's fitting then that James closes his letter not with gushy goodbyes, but with pragmatic instructions to help believers stay close to the truth and experience the power of God.

Digging In

Wandering and Wanderers

Using your Scripture sheets, read James 5:19-20. Mark the two types of people represented in the passage. (You might circle one and underline the other.)

Write in the following space a description of each of the two types you identified. Then reread James 5:19-20, and list everything you learn about each type of person.

Think for a moment about what it might look like to *wander from the truth*. Write four or five actions that might indicate someone is wandering from the truth.

If you begin to notice such actions in Christians, what are some ways you could help *turn a sinner from the error of his way*? Write down four or five ideas.

Then think about it this way: If you were to wander from the truth, what would be your reason?

Cross-Checking

The Bible as a Guardrail

Scripture gives us some red flags that can indicate when someone we know is wandering from the truth, as well as tips on how to turn a sinner from error. As you read the following Bible verses, write what you learn about how someone can stray from the truth.

Exodus 23:2

Judges 2:10-12

Psalm 119:10-11

Luke 21:8

James 1:13-18

James 3:14

As you read the next set of passages, record what you learn about why we should bother helping someone who has strayed from the truth. If you learn anything new about how a person might wander, add this information, too.

Ezekiel 34:1-4, 10 (Though this passage is aimed at the shepherds of Israel, every spiritual leader and discipler can take its message to heart.)

Matthew 18:15-20

1 Peter 4:8-11

Jude 21-23

Taking It Inward

Why Leave the Path?

Let's put it all together. Based on the first set of verses you read, summarize the variety of ways people can wander from the truth.

Based on the second set of verses, summarize how we should help the wanderer return to the path.

Wrapping It Up

Any Wanderers You Know?

You probably noticed the wanderers James referred to were those in the Christian community. ("My brothers, if one of you should wander...") Think for a moment about the students who are currently involved with your ministry. In the first column write the names or initials of students who are showing any of the red flags you saw in the verses you looked up earlier. Also consider any students who were once part of your group but have drifted away. You may want to pull out a student ministry or church directory to help you think of names.

Students	Steps toward Restoration

Now prayerfully run each name through the scriptural steps for bringing a wanderer back to truth. Ask God for the wisdom—which he gives generously—to apply these steps to each unique situation. In the second column, write practical actions you can take to begin the process of restoration.

In the group session your students will also be asked to think about any peers who are wandering from the truth. As you and the group work through this exercise, be open to letting a plan emerge that will help you reach out to those who have gravitated to the fringes of your community of believers.

Finish your prep by selecting the appropriate Teach It guide for your session. (Full Teach It guides are on the CD-ROM accompanying this book.) Then read through the guide so you're familiar with the flow of the session and confident with each exercise. Be sure to allow time for printing or photocopying the Scripture sheets and student journal pages, and pulling together any materials needed. Since this is the last session in your study of James, you'll want to devote a few minutes to a review of the group's experience in James.

Before you close your book, take a few moments to pray for your students and your group session. Pray for those students who may be on the verge of wandering from the truth.

WEB SUPPORT: Web support for *Hear and Do* is available at www.inword.org. With this being the last session, consider using one of the long-term follow-up ideas to help your students make a lifestyle out of the truth they've explored in the book of James. You'll find password information in the Instructions at the front of this book.

1. Materials

For this session each student will need—
- the James 5 Scripture sheet
- the student journal page for Session 12
- his or her own Bible, pen, and notebook

You'll also need—
- a whiteboard and markers
- colored pencils (at least two colors per student)
- a wall-size copy of the Scripture (James 5:19-20)
- examples to share from www.questioningfaith.com

2. Session Intro

GOALS OF SESSION 12
As students experience this session, they will—
- discover not everyone in the James community was in a spiritual-growth mode.
- explore why it's possible to wander from the truth, and understand what we can do to safeguard against the wander factor.
- be challenged to reach out to friends who might be wandering.

PRAYER

OPEN: *WALK-AWAY BRAINSTORM*
Group Interaction: Brainstorm with your students reasons people walk away from the faith.

3. Digging In: *Wandering and Wanderers*

Group Dig: Explore James 5:19-20 and look for the different types of people James talks about.

4. Taking It Inward: *Why Leave the Path?*

Group Interaction: Share with each other the dynamics of the *wanderer* and the *turner*.

5. Cross-Checking: *The Bible as a Guardrail*

Personal Retreat: Explore key passages that explain how one might wander from the truth and why one might want to restore the wanderer.

6. Taking It Inward: *Why Leave the Path?*

Group Interaction: Process with each other the dynamics of helping people who are in danger of wandering from the truth.

7. Wrapping It Up: *Whom Can You Restore?*

Group Interaction: Time to name names and think through ways to help your friends.

Final Thoughts

Encourage students to express how James has helped them make changes in their relationships with God.

1. Materials

For this session each student will need—
- the James 5 Scripture sheet
- the student journal page for Session 12
- his or her own Bible, pen, and notebook

You'll also need—
- a whiteboard and markers
- colored pencils (at least two colors per student)
- a fireplace log or a large stick (slightly charred if not too messy), 3x5 cards, and push pins (at least one per student) for Wrapping It Up
- optional: blank paper for Final Thoughts

2. Session Intro

GOALS OF SESSION 12
As students experience this session, they will—
- discover not everyone in the James community was in a spiritual-growth mode.
- explore why it's possible to wander from the truth, and understand what we can do to safeguard against the wander factor.
- be challenged to reach out to friends who might be wandering.

PRAYER

OPEN: *WALK-AWAY BRAINSTORM*
Group Interaction: Brainstorm with your students reasons people walk away from the faith.

3. Digging In: *Wandering and Wanderers*

Group Dig: Explore James 5:19-20 and look for the different types of people James talks about.

4. Taking It Inward: *Why Leave the Path?*

Group Interaction: Share with each other the dynamics of the *wanderer* and the *turner*.

5. Cross-Checking: *The Bible as a Guardrail*

Personal Retreat: Explore key passages that explain how one might wander from the truth and why one might want to restore the wanderer.

6. Taking It Inward: *Why Leave the Path?*

Group Interaction: Process with each other the dynamics of helping people who are in danger of wandering from the truth.

7. Wrapping It Up: *Whom Can You Restore?*

Group Interaction: Time to name names and think through ways to help your friends.

Final Thoughts

Encourage students to express how James has helped them make changes in their relationships with God.

1. Materials

For this session each student will need—
- the James 5 Scripture sheet
- the student journal page for Session 12
- his or her own Bible, pen, and notebook

You'll also need—
- a whiteboard and markers
- colored pencils (at least two colors per student)
- a loose-leaf ring (you can find these at office supply stores), a hole punch, and 3x5 cards (one or two per student) for Wrapping it Up
- optional: blank paper for Final Thoughts

2. Session Intro

GOALS OF SESSION 12

As students experience this session, they will—
- discover not everyone in the James community was in a spiritual-growth mode.
- explore why it's possible to wander from the truth, and understand what we can do to safeguard against the wander factor.
- be challenged to reach out to friends who might be wandering.

PRAYER

OPEN: *WALK-AWAY BRAINSTORM*
Group Interaction: Brainstorm with your students reasons people walk away from the faith.

3. Digging In: *Wandering and Wanderers*

Group Dig: Explore James 5:19-20 and look for the different types of people James talks about.

4. Taking It Inward: *Why Leave the Path?*

Group Interaction: Share with each other the dynamics of the *wanderer* and the *turner*.

5. Cross-Checking: *The Bible as a Guardrail*

Personal Retreat: Explore key passages that explain how one might wander from the truth and why one might want to restore the wanderer.

6. Taking It Inward: *Why Leave the Path?*

Group Interaction: Process with each other the dynamics of helping people who are in danger of wandering from the truth.

7. Wrapping It Up: *Whom Can You Restore?*

Group Interaction: Time to name names and think through ways to help your friends.

Final Thoughts

Encourage students to express how James has helped them make changes in their relationships with God.

1. Materials

For this session each student will need—
- the James 5 Scripture sheet
- the student journal page for Session 12
- his or her own Bible, pen, and notebook

You'll also need—
- a whiteboard and markers
- colored pencils (at least two colors per student)
- optional: blank paper for Final Thoughts

2. Session Intro

GOALS OF SESSION 12

As students experience this session, they will—
- discover not everyone in the James community was in a spiritual-growth mode.
- explore why it's possible to wander from the truth, and understand what we can do to safeguard against the wander factor.
- be challenged to reach out to friends who might be wandering.

PRAYER

OPEN: *WALK-AWAY BRAINSTORM*
Group Interaction: Brainstorm with your students reasons people walk away from the faith.

3. Digging In: *Wandering and Wanderers*

Group Dig: Explore James 5:19-20 and look for the different types of people James talks about.

4. Taking It Inward: *Why Leave the Path?*

Group Interaction: Share with each other the dynamics of the *wanderer* and the *turner*.

5. Cross-Checking: *The Bible as a Guardrail*

Personal Retreat: Explore key passages that explain how one might wander from the truth and why one might want to restore the wanderer.

6. Taking It Inward: *Why Leave the Path?*

Group Interaction: Process with each other the dynamics of helping people who are in danger of wandering from the truth.

7. Wrapping It Up: *Whom Can You Restore?*

Group Interaction: Time to name names and think through ways to help your friends.

Final Thoughts

Encourage students to express how James has helped them make changes in their relationships with God and look ahead to how they can continue to let what they've learned shape their spiritual lives.

1. Materials

For this session each student will need—
- his or her own Bible and pen
- optional: journal page for Session 12 (Using the student journal page is optional in the coffeehouse setting because table space may be limited.)

You'll also need—
- a pack of pencils with erasers
- optional: a few spare Bibles for students who've forgotten theirs
- optional: blank paper for Final Thoughts

2. Session Intro

GOALS OF SESSION 12

As students experience this session, they will—
- discover not everyone in the James community was in a spiritual-growth mode.
- explore why it's possible to wander from the truth, and understand what we can do to safeguard against the wander factor.
- be challenged to reach out to friends who might be wandering.

PRAYER

OPEN: *WALK-AWAY BRAINSTORM*
Group Interaction: Brainstorm with your students reasons people walk away from the faith.

3. Digging In: *Wandering and Wanderers*

Group Dig: Explore James 5:19-20 and look for the different types of people James talks about.

4. Taking It Inward: *Why Leave the Path?*

Group Interaction: Share with each other the dynamics of the *wanderer* and the *turner*.

5. Cross-Checking: *The Bible as a Guardrail*

Group Dig: Explore key passages that explain how one might wander from the truth and why one might want to restore the wanderer.

6. Taking It Inward: *Why Leave the Path?*

Group Interaction: Process with each other the dynamics of helping people who are in danger of wandering from the truth.

7. Wrapping It Up: *Whom Can You Restore?*

Group Interaction: Time to name names and think through ways to help your friends.

Final Thoughts

Encourage students to express how James has helped them make changes in their relationships with God.

1. Materials (Optional)

- A media presentation featuring your or your students' baby pictures
- A live rescue video from a video-sharing Web site like YouTube. The U.S. Coast Guard probably supplies the best of these. Search words such as: *top 10 Coast Guard rescue.*
- A video clip from the movie *Cliffhanger*: Chapter 2, "Sarah"—DVD counter cues 00:07:37 to 00:09:13

2. Optional Openings

Visual Illustration: Before the session, scan some baby pictures into a PowerPoint presentation. You can play a guess-the-baby game, or just get students to "ooh" and "aah."

Video Clip: Show a few real-life rescues on video. You can find these on video-sharing Web sites such as YouTube.

Video Clip: Show a video clip from the movie *Cliffhanger* with Sylvester Stallone.

Quotations: Share a few quotations about babyhood.

3. Digging In

Personal Story: Share from your personal experience about seeing people make decisions to follow Christ.

4. Digging Deeper

James 5:19-20: We have a responsibility to parent new believers entrusted to our care.

5. Taking It Inward

People will always be tempted to walk away from the faith. And many will walk away. That doesn't mean we shouldn't try to preserve the ones around us. When we reach out to someone wandering from the truth, it's like plucking someone from a capsized boat in a raging sea.

6. Wrapping It Up

Challenge: When our lives demonstrate to others that the gospel works—that it actually makes people better—we've taken the first step in throwing a life preserver.

James 1

1 James, a servant of God and of the Lord Jesus Christ, To the twelve tribes scattered among the nations: Greetings.

2 Consider it pure joy, my brothers, whenever you face trials of many kinds,

3 because you know that the testing of your faith develops perseverance.

4 Perseverance must finish its work so that you may be mature and complete, not lacking anything.

5 If any of you lacks wisdom, he should ask God, who gives generously to all without finding fault, and it will be given to him.

6 But when he asks, he must believe and not doubt, because he who doubts is like a wave of the sea, blown and tossed by the wind.

7 That man should not think he will receive anything from the Lord;

8 he is a double-minded man, unstable in all he does.

9 The brother in humble circumstances ought to take pride in his high position.

10 But the one who is rich should take pride in his low position, because he will pass away like a wild flower.

11 For the sun rises with scorching heat and withers the plant; its blossom falls and its beauty is destroyed. In the same way, the rich man will fade away even while he goes about his business.

12 Blessed is the man who perseveres under trial, because when he has stood the test, he will receive the crown of life that God has promised to those who love him.

13 When tempted, no one should say, "God is tempting me." For God cannot be tempted by evil, nor does he tempt anyone;

14 but each one is tempted when, by his own evil desire, he is dragged away and enticed.

15 Then, after desire has conceived, it gives birth to sin; and sin, when it is full-grown, gives birth to death.

16 Don't be deceived, my dear brothers.

17 Every good and perfect gift is from above, coming down from the Father of the heavenly lights,

who does not change like shifting shadows.

18 He chose to give us birth through the word of truth, that we might be a kind of firstfruits of all he created.

19 My dear brothers, take note of this: Everyone should be quick to listen, slow to speak and slow to become angry,

20 for man's anger does not bring about the righteous life that God desires.

21 Therefore, get rid of all moral filth and the evil that is so prevalent and humbly accept the word planted in you, which can save you.

22 Do not merely listen to the word, and so deceive yourselves. Do what it says.

23 Anyone who listens to the word but does not do what it says is like a man who looks at his face in a mirror

24 and, after looking at himself, goes away and immediately forgets what he looks like.

25 But the man who looks intently into the perfect law that gives freedom, and continues to do this, not forgetting what he has heard, but doing it—he will be blessed in what he does.

26 If anyone considers himself religious and yet does not keep a tight rein on his tongue, he deceives himself and his religion is worthless.

27 Religion that God our Father accepts as pure and faultless is this: to look after orphans and widows in their distress and to keep oneself from being polluted by the world.

James 2

1 My brothers, as believers in our glorious Lord Jesus Christ, don't show favoritism.

2 Suppose a man comes into your meeting wearing a gold ring and fine clothes, and a poor man in shabby clothes also comes in.

3 If you show special attention to the man wearing fine clothes and say, "Here's a good seat for you," but say to the poor man, "You stand there" or "Sit on the floor by my feet,"

4 have you not discriminated among yourselves and become judges with evil thoughts?

5 Listen, my dear brothers: Has not God chosen those who are poor in the eyes of the world to be rich in faith and to inherit the kingdom he promised those who love him?

6 But you have insulted the poor. Is it not the rich who are exploiting you? Are they not the ones who are dragging you into court?

7 Are they not the ones who are slandering the noble name of him to whom you belong?

8 If you really keep the royal law found in Scripture, "Love your neighbor as yourself," you are doing right.

9 But if you show favoritism, you sin and are convicted by the law as lawbreakers.

10 For whoever keeps the whole law and yet stumbles at just one point is guilty of breaking all of it.

11 For he who said, "Do not commit adultery," also said, "Do not murder." If you do not commit adultery but do commit murder, you have become a lawbreaker.

12 Speak and act as those who are going to be judged by the law that gives freedom,

13 because judgment without mercy will be shown to anyone who has not been merciful. Mercy triumphs over judgment!

14 What good is it, my brothers, if a man claims to have faith but has no deeds? Can such faith save him?

15 Suppose a brother or sister is without clothes and daily food.

16 If one of you says to him, "Go, I wish you well; keep warm and well fed," but does nothing about his physical needs, what good is it?

17 In the same way, faith by itself, if it is not accompanied by action, is dead.

18 But someone will say, "You have faith; I have deeds." Show me your faith without deeds, and I will show you my faith by what I do.

19 You believe that there is one God. Good! Even the demons believe that—and shudder.

20 You foolish man, do you want evidence that faith without deeds is useless?

21 Was not our ancestor Abraham considered righteous for what he did when he offered his son Isaac on the altar?

22 You see that his faith and his actions were working together, and his faith was made complete by what he did.

23 And the scripture was fulfilled that says, "Abraham believed God, and it was credited to him as righteousness," and he was called God's friend.

24 You see that a person is justified by what he does and not by faith alone.

25 In the same way, was not even Rahab the prostitute considered righteous for what she did when she gave lodging to the spies and sent them off in a different direction?

26 As the body without the spirit is dead, so faith without deeds is dead.

James 3

1 Not many of you should presume to be teachers, my brothers, because you know that we who teach will be judged more strictly.

2 We all stumble in many ways. If anyone is never at fault in what he says, he is a perfect man, able to keep his whole body in check.

3 When we put bits into the mouths of horses to make them obey us, we can turn the whole animal.

4 Or take ships as an example. Although they are so large and are driven by strong winds, they are steered by a very small rudder wherever the pilot wants to go.

5 Likewise the tongue is a small part of the body, but it makes great boasts. Consider what a great forest is set on fire by a small spark.

6 The tongue also is a fire, a world of evil among the parts of the body. It corrupts the whole person, sets the whole course of his life on fire, and is itself set on fire by hell.

7 All kinds of animals, birds, reptiles and creatures of the sea are being tamed and have been tamed by man,

8 but no man can tame the tongue. It is a restless evil, full of deadly poison.

9 With the tongue we praise our Lord and Father, and with it we curse men, who have been made in God's likeness.

10 Out of the same mouth come praise and cursing. My brothers, this should not be.

11 Can both fresh water and salt water flow from the same spring?

12 My brothers, can a fig tree bear olives, or a grapevine bear figs? Neither can a salt spring produce fresh water.

13 Who is wise and understanding among you? Let him show it by his good life, by deeds done in the humility that comes from wisdom.

14 But if you harbor bitter envy and selfish ambition in your hearts, do not boast about it or deny the truth.

15 Such "wisdom" does not come down from heaven but is earthly, unspiritual, of the devil.

16 For where you have envy and selfish ambition, there you find disorder and every evil practice.

17 But the wisdom that comes from heaven is first of all pure; then peace-loving, considerate, submissive, full of mercy and good fruit, impartial and sincere.

18 Peacemakers who sow in peace raise a harvest of righteousness.

James 4

1   What causes fights and quarrels among you? Don't they come from your desires that battle within you?

2   You want something but don't get it. You kill and covet, but you cannot have what you want. You quarrel and fight. You do not have, because you do not ask God.

3   When you ask, you do not receive, because you ask with wrong motives, that you may spend what you get on your pleasures.

4   You adulterous people, don't you know that friendship with the world is hatred toward God? Anyone who chooses to be a friend of the world becomes an enemy of God.

5   Or do you think Scripture says without reason that the spirit he caused to live in us envies intensely?

6   But he gives us more grace. That is why Scripture says: "God opposes the proud but gives grace to the humble."

7   Submit yourselves, then, to God. Resist the devil, and he will flee from you.

8   Come near to God and he will come near to you. Wash your hands, you sinners, and purify your hearts, you double-minded.

9   Grieve, mourn and wail. Change your laughter to mourning and your joy to gloom.

10 Humble yourselves before the Lord, and he will lift you up.

11 Brothers, do not slander one another. Anyone who speaks against his brother or judges him speaks against the law and judges it. When you judge the law, you are not keeping it, but sitting in judgment on it.

12 There is only one Lawgiver and Judge, the one who is able to save and destroy. But you—who are you to judge your neighbor?

13 Now listen, you who say, "Today or tomorrow we will go to this or that city, spend a year there, carry on business and make money."

14 Why, you do not even know what will happen tomorrow. What is your life? You are a mist that appears for a little while and then vanishes.

15 Instead, you ought to say, "If it is the Lord's will, we will live and do this or that."

16 As it is, you boast and brag. All such boasting is evil.

17 Anyone, then, who knows the good he ought to do and doesn't do it, sins.

James 5

1   Now listen, you rich people, weep and wail because of the misery that is coming upon you.

2   Your wealth has rotted, and moths have eaten your clothes.

3   Your gold and silver are corroded. Their corrosion will testify against you and eat your flesh like fire. You have hoarded wealth in the last days.

4   Look! The wages you failed to pay the workmen who mowed your fields are crying out against you. The cries of the harvesters have reached the ears of the Lord Almighty.

5   You have lived on earth in luxury and self-indulgence. You have fattened yourselves in the day of slaughter.

6   You have condemned and murdered innocent men, who were not opposing you.

7   Be patient, then, brothers, until the Lord's coming. See how the farmer waits for the land to yield its valuable crop and how patient he is for the autumn and spring rains.

8   You too, be patient and stand firm, because the Lord's coming is near.

9   Don't grumble against each other, brothers, or you will be judged. The Judge is standing at the door!

10 Brothers, as an example of patience in the face of suffering, take the prophets who spoke in the name of the Lord.

11 As you know, we consider blessed those who have persevered. You have heard of Job's perseverance and have seen what the Lord finally brought about. The Lord is full of compassion and mercy.

12 Above all, my brothers, do not swear—not by heaven or by earth or by anything else. Let your "Yes" be yes, and your "No," no, or you will be condemned.

13 Is any one of you in trouble? He should pray. Is anyone happy? Let him sing songs of praise.

14 Is any one of you sick? He should call the elders of the church to pray over him and anoint him with oil in the name of the Lord.

15 And the prayer offered in faith will make the sick person well; the Lord will raise him up. If he has

sinned, he will be forgiven.

16 Therefore confess your sins to each other and pray for each other so that you may be healed. The prayer of a righteous man is powerful and effective.

17 Elijah was a man just like us. He prayed earnestly that it would not rain, and it did not rain on the land for three and a half years.

18 Again he prayed, and the heavens gave rain, and the earth produced its crops.

19 My brothers, if one of you should wander from the truth and someone should bring him back,

20 remember this: Whoever turns a sinner from the error of his way will save him from death and cover over a multitude of sins.